The Illustrated Dictionary of Snark

The *Illustrated Dictionary of* Snark

A Snide, Sarcastic Guide to Verbal Sparring, Comebacks, Irony, Insults, and Much More

Lawrence Dorfman

Skyhorse Publishing

Skyhorse Publishing books may be purchased in bulk at special discounts for sales promotion, corporate gifts, fund-raising, or educational purposes. Special editions can also be created to specifications. For details, contact the Special Sales Department, Skyhorse Publishing, 307 West 36th Street, 11th Floor, New York, NY 10018 or info@skyhorsepublishing.com.

Skyhorse® and Skyhorse Publishing® are registered trademarks of Skyhorse Publishing, Inc.®, a Delaware corporation.

Visit our website at www.skyhorsepublishing.com.

10 9 8 7 6 5 4 3 2 1

Library of Congress Cataloging-in-Publication Data is available on file.

ISBN: 978-1-62087-187-4

Printed in China

This book is dedicated to all those snarky folks out there who love a witty comeback, a well-turned line, a pithy bon mot, a great retort, a cut-to-the-quick insult, a clever retort, or a good snark.

Thanks also to a great support staff at Skyhorse and the usual bunch of crazies in my life . . . you know who you are.

And, of course, to RP . . . light at the end of the tunnel that isn't an oncoming train.

CONTENTS

Introduction

When my first Snark book came out some four years ago, the word "snark" was a term that was rarely heard. It was never mentioned on radio or television. It wasn't used to describe a sarcastic website or a bitingly nasty novel or a particularly pithy magazine article.

No. Snark was only used on the somewhat rare occasion when someone needed a word to describe an attitude that was a little more than sarcastic and definitely a lot more than snide. Thus, the term "snark" was born.

It had admittedly been around for a while, lurking about in the staid literary canon where it was used to great effect by Lewis Carrol in *The Hunting of the Snark* and by Jack London in *The Cruise of the Snark*. But in the popular media? Not so much.

So just where did the idea of giving "snark" a rebirth come from?

It started after reading *Snark* by David Denby, a pissy polemic against snark and its uses in the political arena. Denby tried to make the case that snark was beginning to run rampant in the media—ruining conversations and shutting down any real discussion of the issues. As is often the case, his warning not only went unheeded, but in fact played a role in kick-starting its general acceptance.

So shortly after, snark was considered cool and hip. It became the foundation of a generation of comic's jokes and routines. They used it liberally and their often ill-based tirades were little more than attempts to separate themselves from mainstream humor and declare to each other that they were all a part of the same great contemporary group. It became a badge for them, an identity. And soon enough, it became the very mainstream of humor that they have just recently rallied against.

I watched all this with despair. Most of these five-minute wonders had the cutting edge of a plastic knife, and their humor certainly missed more than it hit. There was no genius here, not when compared to the great snarkists/humorists like Dorothy Parker, Groucho Marx, Robert Benchley, Oscar Wilde, H. L. Mencken . . . the list goes on and on.

But I did recognize that there were a few great contemporary wits working in snark. I liked Dennis Leary, Bill Hicks, Bill Maher, Lewis Black, and Dennis Miller. I wanted to celebrate them; to put together an homage to the wit and witticisms of these great snarkists, and thus an idea was hatched.

The topics covered in this book touch on everything snark. We have the use of vitriolic repartee with a sly, knowing, condescending tone to it. We also touch on the words that "hurt so good," with the clever—and sometimes hurtful—insult. Then I thought: *What one thing can cause the greatest amount of snark? What makes people angry and sarcastic and ready to cut their fellow man to the quick?* And then, like a lightning bolt from Zeus, the answer arrived: S-E-X. (Spelled just like that, with the hyphens and everything. Good thing the Greek deity didn't send me ἔρωτας, the

Greek word for sex. Things would have turned out completely different.)

> *The Illustrated Dictionary of Snark* also delves into the sanctity of marriage and family as a whole. To sum up our mindset, we borrow some words from the great, Louis C. K.'s stand up, *Shameless*:

> Divorce is always good news. I know that sounds weird, but it's true because no good marriage has ever ended in divorce. . . . That would be sad. If two people were married and they were really [happy] and they just had a great thing and then they got divorced, that would be really sad. But that has happened zero times.

Politics pundits, clichés, the whole shebang. All these and more are touched on and available in one handy volume. You'll laugh, you'll cry (mostly about spending the money). It'll be a combination of *Cats* and *Les Misérables*, "Stairway to Heaven" and "Freebird," *Jeop-*

ardy and *Wheel of Fortune* all rolled into one . . . but one that conveniently still fits on the back of the toilet seat, to be dipped into time after time during what is the American public's usual reading time. (Caution: The pages are not flushable.)

Robert Hunter once wrote the words, "what a long strange trip it's been" . . . amen brother.
And it ain't over yet!

Lawrence Dorfman

Opposite
Sex

It's better to have loved and lost than never to have loved at all—Nah, not buyin' it, not one lil' bit.

++

Absence makes the heart grow fonder—Is it really the heart? Pretty sure absence makes the . . . hell, I don't know, can't remember now . . . maybe it was "abstinence" . . . what does abstinence make grow again?

+++

She's as beautiful as the day is long—Just remember . . . the day always ends with night . . . dark, terrifying, ugly night. And that can be mighty long, too.

++

You make a better door than a window—Hey, I've always been more of a door man—check out those knockers.

+++

She fell out of the ugly tree and hit every branch on the way down—Clearly, she likes climbing back up there, over and over and over.

✦✦✦

Always a bridesmaid—That should be telling you something.

✦✦

Beat around the bush—Drunken first sexual encounter or some retro political campaign slogan? Your guess.

✦✦✦

Life's a bitch—Then you die . . . or get married.

✦✦

Sweet 16 and never been kissed—She did say "kissed," yes?

✦✦✦

Cat-like grace

✦

It changed his/her life forever

✦

Doesn't know if she's washing or hanging out

✦

A faint heart never a true love knows

✦

Got knocked up

✦

Hanky panky

✦

To your heart's content

✦

Went storming off in a huff

✦

Twist of fate

✦

Fashion victim

✦

Don't upset the apple cart

✦

Don't get your knickers in a twist (English)

✦

Don't trust the lock to which everyone has a key

✦

Give and take

✦

He/she is as dense as a London fog

✦

Meaningful relationship

✦

We're at loggerheads

✦

Significant other

✦

A rose by any other name would smell as sweet—I guess you can call them what you want . . . but I guarantee that sending your wife a dozen American Beauty long stemmed "spider warts" will not get you laid.

✦✦

She's as cold as ice—And twice as slippery. And your tongue always gets stuck to her.

✦✦✦

She's as delicate as a flower—Nothing delicate about that smell, though.

✦✦

You can't buy love—But you can pay heavily for it.

✦✦✦

I've had a perfectly wonderful evening. But this wasn't it.
—GROUCHO MARX

✦✦

Lines Men Use

➢ All those curves, and me with no brakes.

➢ Let's go to my place and do the things I'll tell everyone we did anyway.

➢ Don't worry, it only seems kinky the first time.

➢ You're so fine, you make me want to go out and get a job.

➢ My magical watch says you aren't wearing any panties. Oh, you are? It must be an hour fast!

You cannot make someone love you—All you can do is stalk them and hope they panic, and then give in.

✦✦✦

Women might be able to fake orgasms. But men can fake whole relationships.
—SHARON STONE

✦✦

Excuses to Get Out of a Date[1]

➤ I'm teaching my dog to yodel.

➤ I prefer to remain an enigma. Or a conundrum. I forget which.

➤ Sorry, I'm trying to finish *He's Just Not That Into You.*

➤ My friend is on *The Bachelor* (or *The Bachelorette*) and I promised to stay single during the show in case they needed someone new.

➤ I don't think you can afford the lifestyle I've become accustomed to.

➤ I'm so sorry but my shrink doesn't think you sound right for me.

➤ Drinks are a bad idea; I have an AA appointment that night.

➤ I'm sorry, what did you say? I have a terrible habit of ignoring people who bore me.

---

[1] Snark is the ideal way to form an excuse, as it states something that is (1) impossible or (2) obvious. So if your date buys it, he or she is clearly a moron. And if he or she doesn't buy it, then maybe you should be giving him or her a chance.

Snarky Things You Don't Want to Hear During Sex

- ➤ Twins can feel what's happening to each other and mine just called to complain.
- ➤ Could we do this without kissing? I'm trying to talk on the phone.
- ➤ Could you undress closer to the blinking red light?
- ➤ This is one case where you can't blame the condom.
- ➤ I haven't felt this good since the conjugal visits.

Marriage is not a word. It's a sentence.

✦✦✦

~✦~

Lady Nancy Astor once got annoyed at Churchill. "Winston," she said sharply, "if you were my husband I'd put poison in your coffee." "And if I were your husband," responded Churchill, "I'd drink it."

~✦~

Anyone who believes that men are the equal of women has never seen a man trying to wrap a Christmas present.
—ANONYMOUS

◆◆

Kiss her under the mistletoe? I wouldn't kiss her under anesthetic.

◆◆◆

Why a Christmas Tree Is Better Than a Man

1. A Christmas tree is always erect.

2. Even small ones give satisfaction.

3. A Christmas tree stays up for twelve days and nights.

4. A Christmas tree always looks good—even with the lights on.

5. A Christmas tree is always happy with its size.

6. A Christmas tree doesn't get mad if you break one of its balls.

7. You can throw a Christmas tree out when it's past its sell-by date.

8. You don't have to put up with a Christmas tree all year.

Why a Christmas Tree Is Better Than a Woman

1. A Christmas tree doesn't care how many other Christmas trees you have had in the past.

2. Christmas trees don't get mad if you use exotic electrical devices.

3. A Christmas tree doesn't care if you have an artificial one in the closet.

4. A Christmas tree doesn't get mad if you break one of its balls.

5. You can feel a Christmas tree before you take it home.

6. A Christmas tree doesn't get mad if you look up underneath it.

7. A Christmas tree doesn't get jealous around other Christmas trees.

8. A Christmas tree doesn't care if you watch football all day.

She was a large woman who seemed not so much
dressed as upholstered.[2]
—JAMES MATTHEW BARRIE

✦✦

She was what we used to call a suicide blonde—dyed
by her own hand.
—SAUL BELLOW

✦✦✦

---

[2] This from the guy who wrote *Peter Pan*?

The trouble with her is that she lacks the power of
conversation but not the power of speech.
—GEORGE BERNARD SHAW

◆◆

She has the attention span of a lightning bolt.
—ROBERT REDFORD

◆◆◆

Her figure described a set of parabolas that could
cause cardiac arrest in a yak.
—WOODY ALLEN

◆◆

I treasure every moment I don't see her.
—OSCAR LEVANT on Phyllis Diller

◆◆◆

Kirstie Alley says she makes her new boyfriends wait
six months to have sex with her. Of course, some
insist on twelve months.
—CONAN O'BRIEN

◆◆

Snarkin' the News

↔ Doesn't it sometimes feel like you're in the middle of a joke? Three women were arrested for showing up at a drug hearing carrying drugs. Included was a tourniquet, a syringe, a copious amount of pills, and some hash. Why not wear T-shirts that say "We have drugs"? Did they think the term "drug test" was going to be an oral exam? Or that the authorities would test their drugs for them, you know, for quality? Yikes.

↔ A group of Hasidic women chased down a twelve-year-old mugger, took his gun, and held him until the police came. When they finally arrived, the boy screamed, "Please, please take me to jail. I can't stand the guilt anymore!"

↔ "My wife just had a baby." "Congratulations! Whose is it?"[3]

---

[3] Joe Frazier to Ken Norton

Things Men Would Do with a Vagina for a Day

1. Immediately go shopping for cucumbers and zucchini.

2. Squat over a handheld mirror for an hour.

3. See if it's possible to launch a ping-pong ball twenty feet.

4. Finally find that damned G-spot.

Things Women Would Do with a Penis for a Day

1. Get ahead faster in corporate America.

2. Get a blow job.

3. Pee standing.

4. Jump up and down naked with an erection to see if it feels as funny as it looks.

5. Repeat number 2.

~✦~

When her husband passed away, the wife put the usual death notice in the newspaper, but added that he had died of gonorrhea. Once the daily newspapers had been delivered, a good friend of the family phoned and complained bitterly, "You know very well that he died of diarrhea, not gonorrhea."

Replied the widow, "Yes, I know that he died of diarrhea, but I thought it would be better for posterity to remember him as a great lover rather than the big shit that he really was."

~✦~

If you want to know how your girl will treat you after marriage, just listen to her talking to her little brother.

—SAM LEVENSON

✦✦

Sexual Indiscretions Match Box[4]

A. John Edwards   D. Larry Craig
B. Amy Fisher   E. David Letterman
C. Marv Albert   F. Elizabeth Taylor

~♦~

1. A sportscaster who became the butt of jokes when he was accused of sodomy and other bizarre sexual proclivities by a woman with whom he had a decade-long affair. His longtime girlfriend stood by him, and they recently married. That's what I call true love.

2. This movie star was married eight times to seven husbands. When her third husband died, she married his best friend (who was already married to someone else). They divorced; she married another film star whom she divorced, remarried, and divorced again. Two more to go.[5]

---

[4] 1. C, 2. F, 3. D, 4. B, 5. A, 6. E
[5] When you can't sleep, count her husbands.

3. A married senator, with a strong antigay platform, allegedly caught in an airport men's room using his foot to tap out sexual preferences to the FBI agent in the next stall. He says he was just picking up a piece of paper.[6]

4. A complete unknown, she entered into a love tryst at seventeen with a thirty-six-year-old married mechanic and then shot and seriously injured his wife. Also had a sex tape. Still unknown.

5. A strong family-values presidential candidate, he was the subject of a sex tape with his mistress, who was pregnant with his love child at the time. Meanwhile, his wife was dying of cancer. Whaddaya think of those values?

6. After being outed by a news staffer, this married television host and comedian confessed to finding his fun at the office through affairs with several members of his staff.

---

[6] Yeah, a mash note.

LOVE BEFORE SEX

"First comes *love*, then comes *marriage* . . ?" What's the next line? Ah, yes: "Then comes baby in the baby carriage." Now if that doesn't make your toes curl, you're reading the wrong book. Sure, the idea of love before sex is lovely, if antiquated. I'll bet you think that you'll still love your spouse when he or she is ninety-three. You won't even notice how large those underpants are getting—that is, when you actually have a chance to peer into the great canyon that once smartly connected two halves of a tight ass. Even your granny will tell you that falling in love blinds you, that having sex while blind may heighten your sensations,[7] and that heightened sensations lead to marriage, which leads to a baby in a baby carriage. 'Nuff said.

Love is an electric blanket with somebody else in control of the switch.[8]
—CATHY CARLYLE

My wife is pregnant—she took seriously what was poked at her in fun.

✦

Love and eggs are best when fresh.

My wife wants Olympic sex — every four years.

✦

My wife only has sex with me for a purpose. Last night it was to time an egg.

---

[7] Stay with me. There's a point here, somewhere.

[8] It's why love never survives outdoors in the rain.

Love is blind but marriage is a real eye-opener.

✦

Love,
the quest; marriage,
the conquest;
divorce,
the inquest.

✦

Her kisses left something to be desired—the rest of her.

Marry at twenty and you'll be shocked at who you're living with at thirty.

✦

Love is only a dirty trick played on us to achieve continuation of the species.

—W. SOMERSET MAUGHAM

By all means marry; if you get a good wife, you'll be happy. If you get a bad one, you'll become a philosopher.

—SOCRATES

✦

Love at first sight is one of the greatest labor-saving devices the world has ever seen.

Romantic love is . . . a drug. It distorts reality, and that's the point of it. It would be impossible to fall in love with someone you really saw.

—FRAN LEBOWITZ

Until I got married, I was my own worst enemy.

In Pursuit of Sex, Men Will . . .

➤ GO SHOE SHOPPING—"No, they're very different than the seven other pairs in brown you looked at. I completely get the nuance of ecru."

➤ CLEAN THE BATHROOM—"I love the smell of Pine-Sol in the morning . . . smells like . . . cleanliness. And I will definitely put all three hundred of your products back where they were."

➤ WATCH THE NEIGHBOR'S KIDS—"Cool! Now I finally have a reason to watch six hours of *SpongeBob SquarePants* and *Veggie Tales*."

➤ EAT HEALTHY—"Yes, please bring me another helping of that spinach-kale-broccoli-asparagus salad shit, er . . . I mean, wow, tastes amazing!"

➤ THROW AWAY PICTURES OF OLD GIRLFRIENDS—"No, babe, I threw those away. That box way up on that shelf in the garage that you can't reach is all the birthday cards you've sent me."

➤ WATCH A CHICK FLICK—"No, I really do think that Julia Roberts or Sandra Bullock or Natalie Portman *is* the modern-day Clint Eastwood. Love to go."

➤ HAVE DINNER AT HER MOTHER'S—"Of course, it's been too long since I examined every fault I have. I can play poker with the guys anytime."

➤ NOT LAUGH AT TASTELESS JOKES— "Not funny. After all, blondes have feelings too. I'm appalled."

➤ GO GROCERY SHOPPING—"Sure, I'll get your tampons and Midol. If I can't find the size box you need, I can always ask the clerk."

➤ DRESS UP TO GO OUT, EVEN THOUGH IT'S NOT A WEDDING OR A FUNERAL— "Yeah, this suit makes me feel great, babe. It's just like being back at work."

➤ WATCH JIMMY FALLON INSTEAD OF LETTERMAN—"I can totally see it now: He *is* cuter."

➤ ADMIT A MISTAKE—(Hey, let's not get carried away. After all, it's only sex . . . only sex . . . only . . .) "Totally my fault, hon. Won't happen again."

How to Seduce Your Wife:

Compliment her, cuddle her, kiss her, caress her, stroke her, tease her, comfort her, protect her, hug her, hold her, wine and dine her, buy things for her, listen to her, care for her, stand by her, support her, buy flowers for her, go to the ends of the earth for her . . .

How to Seduce Your Husband:

Show up naked. Bring beer.

Things Not to Say During Sex

> - Well, so much for mouth-to-mouth.
> - Hope you're as good looking when I'm sober . . .
> - Do you get any premium movie channels?
> - Try not to smear my makeup . . .
> - Got any penicillin?
> - I thought you had the keys to the handcuffs!

I bought my wife a sex manual but half the pages were missing. We went straight from foreplay to postnatal depression.
—BOB MONKHOUSE

✦✦

So heavy is the chain of wedlock that it needs two to carry it, and sometimes three.
—ALEXANDRE DUMAS[9]

✦✦✦

Things Not to Say During Sex

➢ You woke me up for that?

➢ Do you smell something burning?

➢ Try breathing through your nose.

➢ Can you please pass me the remote control?

➢ On second thought, let's turn off the lights.

➢ And to think—I was trying to pick up your friend!

---

[9] Whole new perspective on *The Three Musketeers*; no?

Things NOT to Say at a Wedding

1. Hey, I think I saw that same dress at Costco!

2. What's the over/under on whether this one will take?

3. Gonna be some ugly kids, no?

4. Get a load of the brides/groom's mom . . . Thanksgiving's gonna be a hoot.

5. I hope they love the vibrator I gave them.

6. Who catered this, Taco Bell?

7. Hopefully there'll be his and her bathrooms and his won't have any mirrors.

8. It's a fairytale wedding—and her mom gets to be the ogre.

9. Is that a bump? Maybe we need to throw puffed rice.

10. His marriage vows will be silence and poverty.

11. It's not that he's going to live longer; it's just going to seem longer.

12. You know how many hookers he could have had for what this wedding costs?

13. What a fastidious couple. She's fast and he's hideous.

My wife and I were happy for twenty years. Then we met.
—RODNEY DANGERFIELD
♦♦

A woman tries to get all she can out of a man, and a man tries to get all he can into a woman.
—ISAAC GOLDBERG
♦♦♦

~♦~

A woman goes to a doctor complaining about knee pains. "Do you indulge in any activities that puts pressure on your knees?" asks the doctor. "Well, my husband and I do it doggy style every night." "I see," said the doctor. "You know, there are other sexual positions." "Not if you want to watch TV, there ain't."

~♦~

Sex Is . . .

➤ Sex is like death, only after death you don't feel like a pizza.

—WOODY ALLEN

✦✦✦

➤ Sex is like art. Most of it is pretty bad, and the good stuff is out of your price range.

—SCOTT ROEBEN

✦✦

➤ Sex is like money. Only too much is enough.

—JOHN UPDIKE

✦✦✦

➤ Sex is kicking death in the ass while singing.

—CHARLES BUKOWSKI

✦✦

➤ Sex is a beautiful thing between two people. Between five, it's fantastic.

—WOODY ALLEN

✦✦✦

➤ Sex is conversation carried out by other means.
—PETER USTINOV
♦♦

➤ Sex is. There's nothing to be done about it.
—ANONYMOUS
♦♦♦

If you made a list of the reasons why any couple got
married, and another list of the reasons for their
divorce, you'd have a hell of a lot of overlapping.
—MIGNON MCLAUGHLIN
♦♦♦

Men don't realize that if we're sleeping with them on
the first date, we're probably not interested in seeing
them again either.
—CHELSEA HANDLER
♦♦

Love is not the dying moan of a distant violin—it's
the triumphant twang of a bedspring.
—S. J. PERELMAN
♦♦♦

WOMEN ON MEN

When you think about the relationship between men and women, it's amazing that more men aren't killed in their sleep. Women deserve a medal for putting up with all the foibles, failings, and folderol that is truly at the heart of those creatures known as *Homo hominis*. We cheat, lie, flirt, cavort, leave the seat up, forget to call, forget to text . . . up to the minute that sex is involved. Then we find we have the memory of an elephant. Women communicate differently than men, cutting through the haze to get to the meat of the matter. Their brains are bigger, they react to stress better . . . but, like men, need to blow off steam regularly. Snark is the perfect tool. The following are examples of the steam that's been shot out in the past. Careful . . . don't get burned.

I married beneath me. All women do.
—NANCY ASTOR

That useless piece of flesh at the end of a penis is a man.
—JO BRAND

When I think of the men I've slept with— if they were women—I wouldn't even have lunch with them.
—CAROL SUSSKIND

The difference between savings bonds and men? At some point, the bonds mature.

✦

Springtime reminds me of the ex. Especially when I'm pruning out the dead wood.

✦

If your husband and a lawyer were drowning and you had to choose, would you go to lunch or to a movie?

I'm not your type. I'm not inflatable.

✦

Women have their faults. Men have only two: Everything they say. Everything they do.

We have a reason to believe that man first walked upright to free his hands for masturbation.

—LILY TOMLIN

Adam came first . . . but then, men always do.

Not all men are annoying. Some are dead.

✦

Sex is like snow, you never know how many inches you're going to get or how long it will last.

✦

Jesus was a typical man. They always say they'll come back, but you never see them again.

✦

What do men and mascara have in common? They both run at the first sign of emotion.

A ring around the finger does not cause a nerve block to the genitals.

✦

If vibrators could light the barbecue or kill spiders in the bathtub, would we need men at all?

—KATHY LETTE

Let's not complicate our relationship by trying to communicate with each other.

✦

Oral sex is like being attacked by a giant snail.
—GERMAINE GREER

✦

If you want to sacrifice the admiration of many men for the criticism of one, go ahead, get married.
—KATHARINE HEPBURN

Love isn't blind, it's retarded.

✦

To marry once is a duty; twice a folly; thrice is madness.

MARRIAGE IS A ROMANCE IN WHICH THE HEROINE DIES IN THE FIRST CHAPTER.
—CECILIA EGAN

He is every other inch a gentleman.
—REBECCA WEST

MEN ON WOMEN

The battle of the sexes rages on. And boy, is everyone pissed or what? Men always think they get the short end of the stick. (Maybe I should rephrase?) How about . . . men always feel they get the shaft. (Nope, not working.)

Anyway, if you're not getting any, your snark meter will be turned up to 11. These are a few of my favorite snarks . . . from the male point of view.

A man is as old as the women he feels.
—GROUCHO MARX

Men have more problems than women. In the first place, they have to put up with women.
—FRANCOISE SAGAN

A DYSLEXIC MAN WALKS INTO A BRA...

I have no luck with women. I once went on a date and asked the woman if she'd brought any protection. She pulled a switchblade on me.
—SCOTT ROEBEN

Every so often, I try to masturbate a large word into conversation, even if I'm not really sure what it means.

✦

Spouse: Someone who'll stand by you through all the trouble you wouldn't have had if you'd stayed single.

To me, a woman's body is a temple. I try to attend services as often as I can.
—WILL SHRINER

✦

I think sex is better than logic, but I can't prove it.

✦

Woman was God's second mistake.
—FRIEDRICH NIETZSCHE

How do you know if it's time to wash the dishes and clean your house? Look inside your pants. If there's a penis there, it's not time.

What men desire is a virgin who is a whore.

Love is very deep, but sex only has to go a few inches.

No matter how good she looks, some other guy is sick and tired of putting up with her shit.

Men say of women what pleases them; women do with men what pleases them.

There's one consolation about matrimony. When you look around you can always see somebody who did worse.

—WARREN H. GOLDSMITH

Ah, women. They make the highs higher and the lows more frequent.

—FRIEDRICH NIETZSCHE

I'm all for bringing back the birch, but only between consenting adults.

—GORE VIDAL

When making love, most married men fantasize that their wives aren't fantasizing.

Love: the sickest of Irony's sick jokes. The place where logic and order go to die.

—CHRISTOPHER MOORE

*

Some don't prefer the pursuit of happiness to the happiness of pursuit.

THE MOST HAPPY MARRIAGE I CAN PICTURE OR IMAGINE TO MYSELF WOULD BE THE UNION OF A DEAF MAN TO A BLIND WOMAN.

—SAMUEL TAYLOR COLERIDGE

I'm always looking for meaningful one night stands.

—DUDLEY MOORE

Falling in love is so hard on the knees.

—AEROSMITH

Things Not to Say During Sex

- ➤ I wish we got the *Playboy* channel . . .
- ➤ But my cat always sleeps on that pillow.
- ➤ Did I tell you my aunt died in this bed?
- ➤ No, really . . . I do this part better myself!
- ➤ It's nice being in bed with a woman I don't have to inflate!
- ➤ This would be more fun with a few more people . . .
- ➤ So much for the fulfillment of sexual fantasies!
- ➤ I think you have it on backwards.
- ➤ When is this supposed to feel good?
- ➤ You're good enough to do this for a living!
- ➤ Is that blood on the headboard?
- ➤ Are you sure I don't know you from somewhere?

There's nothing better than good sex . . . but bad sex? A peanut-butter-and-jelly sandwich is better than bad sex.
—BILLY JOEL

++

Told her the thing I loved most about her was her mind . . . because that's what told her to get into bed with me.
—STEVEN WRIGHT

+++

I like my wine like my women—ready to pass out.
—ROBIN WILLIAMS

++

She's more interested in spice than spouse.

+++

~+~

A man and a woman are lying in bed after a disappointing round of sex. "You've got a very small organ," says the woman. The man replies, "Yeah, well, I didn't know I'd be playing Carnegie Hall."

~+~

Things Not to Say During Sex

- Does this count as a date?

- Have you seen *Fatal Attraction?*

- Sorry about the tags; I'm not very good with names.

- Don't mind me . . . I always file my nails in bed.

- I hope I didn't forget to turn the gas oven off. Do you have a light?

- You could at least *act* like you're enjoying it!

~♦~

Q: What's the difference between a bar and a clitoris?
A: Most men have no trouble finding a bar.

~♦~

He's handsome. When she wants money, he has to hand some over.

♦♦♦

Their marriage is a partnership—he's the silent partner.

♦♦

Euphemisms for Losing Your Virginity

- ➢ Throwing out the first pitch
- ➢ Moving out of Palmdale
- ➢ Learning to work the childproof containers
- ➢ Serving cherry delight
- ➢ Presenting Mr. Happy the key to the Furry City
- ➢ Finally having your weapon inspected
- ➢ Removing the training wheels from the pie cycle
- ➢ Taking the NasTea plunge
- ➢ Getting the VIP tour at Neverland
- ➢ Attending the Bush Inaugural Ball
- ➢ Fornication for $1,000, Alex
- ➢ Landing the Martian probe on Venus

WOMEN ON WOMEN

You can make the argument quite easily that there is no one snarkier than a woman discussing sex—especially when she's talking to another woman about women. You see, though the average heterosexual woman would be loath to admit to a man that she takes . . . a while . . . to climax . . . when she's talking about her inner oyster to another woman, the snarks can fly. Sisterhood, grrl power, feminist doctrine . . . when it comes to speaking frankly, women rule the roost. Take a look.

Now, many of you out there will claim that I added this chapter for myself. Not true. I added this chapter for all the men reading this.

It's so tiring to make love to women; it takes forever. I'm too lazy to be a lesbian.
—CAMILLE PAGLIA

Making love to a woman is like real estate—location, location, location.
—CAROL LEIFER

Some women can't say the word "lesbian"— even when their mouth is full of one.
—KATE CLINTON

Show me a woman who doesn't feel some guilt after sex, and I'll show you a man.
—ERICA JONG

Lead me not into temptation. I can find the way myself.
—RITA MAE BROWN

If male homosexuals are called "gay," then female homosexuals should be called "ecstatic."

—SHELLEY ROBERTS

It's a cosmic joke that I'm a lesbian, because I understand men so well but women are a complete mystery to me.
—LEA DELARIA

We are secretly glad Anne Heche is back on your team. She scares us.

She's not gay. She just ran out of men.

MEN ON MEN

Unlike women who can stay completely open to all the possibilities that might be found in a sexual adventure within their own gender, most men tend to shy away from these trysts. Sometimes vehemently. On top of which, men would rather have a root canal than discuss their own sex life.

While most men love to have sex and many even love to watch it . . . the last thing men want to do is talk about it. At least in any way that isn't bragging, boasting, or macho posturing. Feelings? Emotions? Nah. Leave that to the fairer sex . . . and how about them Bears?

It is impossible to obtain a conviction for sodomy from an English jury. Half of them don't believe that it can physically be done, and the other half is doing it.

—WINSTON CHURCHILL

I'm glad I'm not bisexual—I couldn't stand being rejected by men as well as women.

—BERNARD MANNING

If you have sex with your clone, are you gay or are you masturbating?

+

Why is it so hard to find men who are sensitive and caring? Because those men already have boyfriends.

+

Spaghetti is straight too— until you heat it up.

My cousin is an agoraphobic homosexual, which makes it kind of hard for him to come out of the closet.

—BILL KELLY

The guy runs a prison. He can have any piece of ass he wants.

—*ARRESTED DEVELOPMENT*

It's just a penis, right? Probably no worse for you than smoking.

—DAVID SEDARIS

~◆~

News flash: A man just flashed three women who were sitting on a bench. Two had a stroke but the other couldn't reach.

~◆~

He should have known she was jealous—she had male bridesmaids.

◆◆◆

His towels are monogrammed—His, Hers, and Next.

◆◆

He's the salt of the earth—she's been trying to shake him forever.

◆◆◆

Terminal bachelor—footloose and fiancé free.

◆◆

Always look before you lip.

✦✦✦

My wife stopped pretending to have orgasms years ago. That's all right with me, though, because it allowed me to stop pretending that I cared.
—MIKE RANSTON

✦✦

MATRIMONIAL-HARMONICS.

SEX BEFORE LOVE

Remember that childhood ditty I mentioned earlier? "First comes *love*, then comes *marriage*..?" Is it really a simple song from the playground or a life sentence? Either way, it's wrong. First comes sex. Stop there. Used to be—for women, or so everyone thought—that love and *sex* were inseparable. Couldn't have one without the other. Went together like bread and butter, sugar and spice, Martin and Lewis (?)... well, you know, stuff that goes together. In order to indulge in that one most intimate thing between two people, there needed to be love... (sigh). Well, new day, new rules. Women of today are the same as men of forever... that sex and love don't always have to be in the same room and still everybody still wins. Men have always only needed a time and a place. Anytime and anyplace. Women, welcome to the club. It's a pleasure to have you.

Sex is the most beautiful thing that can take place between a happily married man and his secretary.

— BARRY HUMPHRIES

A man can sleep around, no questions asked, but if a woman makes nineteen or twenty mistakes she's a tramp.

—CAROL SUSSKIND

Love is a matter of chemistry, but sex is a matter of physics.

"You're what?!?" is the most common form of marriage proposal.

BED IS THE POOR MAN'S OPERA.

Sex is like food: when you abstain, even the worst begins to look good.

+

The last thing I want to do is hurt you. But it's still on the list.

Will have sex for self-esteem.

+

Be naughty, save Santa a trip.

Sex on the whole was meant to be short, nasty, and brutish. If what you want is cuddling . . . buy a puppy.

—JULIE BURCHILL

A woman occasionally is quite a serviceable substitute for masturbation.

Sex is like math: you add the bed, subtract the clothes, divide the legs and pray you don't multiply!

—Feras Yaghmour

Things Not to Say During Sex

- ➤ You're almost as good as my ex!
- ➤ You look younger than you feel.
- ➤ Perhaps you're just out of practice.
- ➤ And to think, I didn't even have to buy you dinner!
- ➤ I have a confession . . .
- ➤ I'll tell you whom I'm fantasizing about if you tell me whom you're fantasizing about . . .
- ➤ Petroleum jelly or no petroleum jelly, I said no.
- ➤ Keep it down . . . my mother is a light sleeper . . .
- ➤ My old girlfriend used to do it a *lot* longer!

My wife used to love to talk to me during sex. The other day she called me from a motel.
—RODNEY DANGERFIELD

✦✦

Seven Kinds of Sex

> SMURF SEX—The first throes of passion, when you're fucking until you're blue in the face.

> KITCHEN SEX—You're definitely a couple, but you're still attracted enough to be overcome with desire while making dinner.

> BEDROOM SEX—Her thong has become a brief, he's wearing pajamas, and you usually have sex in bed.

> RELIGIOUS SEX—Nun in the morning, nun in the afternoon, and nun at night.

> HALLWAY SEX—You've been together too long. When you pass each other in the hallway, you say fuck you.

> COURTROOM SEX—Your soon-to-be ex-wife and her lawyer screw you in divorce court in front of many people and for every penny you've got.

> SOCIAL SECURITY SEX—Back in the game, you now get a little each month. But it's not enough to live on.

Religion and God

Bite the dust / Bite your lip / Bite the bullet / Bite your tongue—Come on, bite something already, anything.

+++

Ashes to ashes, dust to dust—Not to mention a few bone fragments, a ligament or two . . . all things visceral, Sherlock.

++

I'm going to hell in a hand basket—Personally, I was hoping for a limo. Not a lot of room in a hand basket and I'm definitely bringin' a few folks with me.

+++

It's better to have loved and lost than never to have loved at all—Nah, not buyin' it, not one lil' bit.

++

Is the Pope Catholic?—Yeah, yeah . . . and the bear shits in woods and a chicken has lips . . . although, some Vatican watchers may actually question that first one.

+++

Close only counts in horseshoes

✦

Cope with grief

✦

Years young

✦

Don't fly off the handle

✦

Everything's copasetic

✦

Final goodbyes

✦

God help us

✦

Existential angst

✦

Moment of glory

✦

Twilight years

✦

Up the creek

✦

What comes around, goes around

✦

Life and limb

✦

Spring to life

✦

Take it easy

✦

Take the plunge

✦

These things happen

✦

Trials and tribulations

✦

Shallow grave

Don't look back, the Devil might be gaining—
Doesn't really matter if you look back or not, he's
pretty much got this race all sewn up.

✦✦✦

Idle hands are the devil's workshop—Boy, you should
see what he can make in that shop . . . no chintzy
little magazine rack for this guy. No, sir.

♦♦♦

He bought the farm—And this is an expression
for dying? Old MacDonald had a farm and then a
massive coronary and "bought the farm." Nice.

♦♦

Make it down and dirty—Despite paying $10,000 for
a coffin, it's the way we're all going to end up. Down
and dirty. No other way TO make it.

♦♦♦

~♦~

Q: Why do only 30 percent of men get into heaven?
A: If it were more, it would be hell.

~♦~

I'm a born-again atheist.
—GORE VIDAL

♦♦♦

I'm still an atheist, thank God.
—LUIS BUÑUEL

++

Pray, *v.* To ask that the laws of the universe be annulled in behalf of a single petitioner confessedly unworthy.
—AMBROSE BIERCE

+++

They always throw around this term the *liberal elite.* And I kept thinking to myself about the Christian right. What's more elite than believing that only you will go to heaven?
—JON STEWART

++

Every day people are straying away from the church and going back to God.
—LENNY BRUCE

+++

~✦~

Jews do not recognize Jesus as the Messiah, Prot-estants do not recognize the pope as the leader of the Christian church, and Baptists do not recog-nize each other in the liquor store or at Hooters.

~✦~

I am prepared to meet my Maker. Whether my Maker is prepared for the great ordeal of meeting me is another matter.
—WINSTON CHURCHILL

✦✦✦

It's not that I'm afraid to die. I just don't want to be there when it happens.
—WOODY ALLEN

✦✦

I have never killed a man, but I have read many obituaries with great pleasure.
—CLARENCE DARROW

✦✦✦

On my gravestone, I want it to say, "I told you I was sick."
—TOM WAITS
♦♦

Probably the worst thing about being Jewish during Christmastime is shopping, because the lines are so long. They should have a Jewish express line. "Look, I'm a Jew. It's not a gift. It's just paper towels!"
—SUE KOLINSKY
♦♦♦

Snark Doctrine

> Taoism: Shit happens.

> Buddhism: If shit happens, it isn't really shit.

> Islam: If shit happens, it is the will of Allah.

> Catholicism: If shit happens, you deserve it.

> Judaism: Why does this shit always happen to us?

> Atheism: I don't believe this shit.

Snarky Ways to Begin a Eulogy

➢ So who else was written out of the will?

➢ Looks like I won the time-of-death pool.

➢ Next time someone says, "Call a doctor," I won't assume it's a joke.

➢ This really doesn't surprise me in a family that considers *Goodfellas* a date film.

➢ I guess that was the main circuit breaker after all.

~♦~

A woman was driving down the street in a sweat because she had an important meeting and couldn't find a parking place. Looking up toward heaven, she said, "Lord, take pity on me. If you find me a parking place, I will go to church every Sunday for the rest of my life and give up sex and tequila." Miraculously, a parking place appeared. She looked up again and said, "Never mind. I found one."

~♦~

Snark at a Funeral

> ➢ Tell the widow she looks hot in black.

> ➢ Tell the undertaker your dog also died and ask can you sneak him into the casket.

> ➢ Punch the body and tell people he hit you first.

> ➢ Ask someone to take a Polaroid of you shaking hands with the deceased.

> ➢ Tell the widow you're the deceased's gay lover.

There ain't no devil; it's just god when he's drunk.
—TOM WAITS

✦✦

~✦~

A woman goes to the post office to buy stamps for her Chanukah cards. She says to the clerk, "May I have 50 Chanukah stamps?" The clerk says, "What denomination?" The woman says, "Oh my god. Has it come to this? Give me 6 Orthodox, 12 Conservative, and 32 Reform."

~✦~

Jesus never put up a tree and exchanged gifts or left cookies out for Santa. He never made a harried last-minute trip to the mall or spent Christmas Eve cursing at a toy he couldn't put together. He celebrated Passover. So if you want to be more like Jesus, pass the matzo.
—DREW CAREY

♦♦

I sometimes think that God, in creating man, somewhat overestimated his ability.
—OSCAR WILDE

♦♦♦

He is useless on top of the ground; he ought to be under it, inspiring the cabbages.
—MARK TWAIN

♦♦

If you can't be a good example, then you'll just have to
be a horrible warning.
—CATHERINE AIRD

♦♦

He would make a lovely corpse.
—CHARLES DICKENS

♦♦♦

He is an old bore. Even the grave yawns for him.
—HERBERT BEERBOHM TREE

♦♦

To hear religious people talk, one would think God
created the torso, head, legs, and arms, but the devil
slapped on the genitals.
—DON SCHRADER

♦♦♦

You know why God is a man? Because if God was
a woman, she would have made sperm taste like
chocolate.
—CARRIE SNOW

♦♦

Things Not to Say at a Funeral

↔ I should have said something earlier . . . but I really, really need his kidney.

↔ Whoa. I didn't know we were supposed to dress up.

↔ You look like you've seen a ghost.

↔ Boy, you wouldn't believe the day I'm having.

↔ Pull my finger.

↔ See, kids? This is what God does to the bad ones.

↔ Who needs gum?

I've learned a lot about women. I think I've learned exactly how the fall of man occurred in the Garden of Eden. Adam and Eve were in the Garden of Eden, and Adam said one day, "Wow, Eve, here we are, at one with nature, at one with God. We'll never age, we'll never die, and all our dreams come true the instant that we have them." And Eve said, "Yeah . . . it's just not enough, is it?"

—BILL HICKS

◆◆

Match the Person to His Final Words[10]

A. Louis B. Mayer   D. Humphrey Bogart
B. Lady Nancy Astor   E. James W. Rodgers
C. Carl Panzram   F. Winston Churchill

~✦~

1. I should never have switched from Scotch to martinis.

2. I'm bored with it all.

3. Hurry it up you Hoosier bastard! I could hang a dozen men while you're screwing around.

4. Am I dying, or is this my birthday?

5. It wasn't worth it.

6. A bulletproof vest. (Asked if he has any last requests before facing a firing squad.)

---

[10] 1. D. , 2. F., 3. C., 4. B., 5. A., 6. E.

Epitaphs

Here lies my wife: here let her lie. Now she's at rest and so am I.
—JOHN DRYDEN

+++

Where his soul's gone or how it fares; nobody knows, and nobody cares.
—ANONYMOUS

++

Hotten Rotten Forgotten
—on JOHN HOTTEN

+++

~+~

Two nuns ride their bikes down a lane. The first nun says, "I've never come this way before!" The second nun says, "Oh, it must be the cobblestone."

~+~

God created sex. Priests created marriage.
—VOLTAIRE

++

The Bible contains 6 admonishments to homosexuals and 362 admonishments to heterosexuals. That doesn't mean that God doesn't love heterosexuals. It's just that they need more supervision.

—LYNN LAVNER

✦✦✦

Conflict

You have to turn the other cheek—What . . . and get that one slapped, too? Okay, c'mon, I'm a man, I can take it. Hey!! Not so hard.

✦✦✦

His bark is worse than the bite—Really? Given how much of a jerk-off he is, that must be some frickin' bark.

✦✦

Curiosity killed the cat—Well, really, what did that cat expect, after waking Curiosity up at that hour of the morning and jumping on the bed, while trying to get under the covers?

✦✦✦

I want to kill two birds with one stone—Try tying the two of them together with weighted rocks . . . works like a charm every time.

✦✦

He who lives by the sword shall die by the sword—
Of course, a machine gun is so much faster and
makes a point so much better . . . right, Scarface?

✦✦✦

The pen is mightier than the sword—Not sure who
you've been fighting with but I'm not going up against
a swordsman with a Paper Mate—not now, not never.

✦✦

I could do that with one hand tied behind my back—
Sure you can, as long as you've got a gun in the other
hand.

✦✦✦

I have an axe to grind—Hey, you'll find it so much
more rewarding when you actually swing it . . .
Grinding it is just tedious. Just ask Lizzie Borden.

✦✦

Don't beat yourself up—even though I can see how incredibly easy, and TEMPTING, it might be to do it.

✦✦✦

This hurts me worse than it does you—Uh, no, scratch that . . . this is definitely gonna hurt you WAY more than it does me.

✦✦

Far be it from me—which is exactly where I'd like to
be, far be it from you.

✦✦✦

He rushes into a fight with the horns of a bull and
the skin of a rabbit.
—JEREMIAH BLACK [on James Garfield]

✦✦

People say I'm ruthless. I am not ruthless . . . and if I
find the SOB that's calling me ruthless, I will destroy
him.
—BOBBY KENNEDY

✦✦✦

Al Gore is like the fat boy in the schoolyard.
Tormenting him is so much fun, nobody can resist
. . . a natural-born victim.
—RUSSELL BAKER

✦✦

Winston Churchill would kill his own mother just so he could use her skin to make a drum to beat his own praises.
—MARGOT ASQUITH

+++

Filthy storyteller, despot, liar, thief, braggart, buffoon, usurper, monster, ignoramus Abe, old scoundrel, perjurer, swindler, tyrant, field-butcher, land-pirate . . .
—*HARPERS MAGAZINE* [on Abraham Lincoln]

++

My hope is that gays will be running the world, because then there would be no war. Just a greater emphasis on military apparel.
—ROSEANNE BARR

+++

A prisoner of war is a man who tries to kill you and
fails, and then asks you not to kill him.
—WINSTON CHURCHILL

+ +

I detest war; it ruins conversation.
—BERNARD FONTENELLE

+ + +

They hardly make 'em like him anymore—but just to
be on the safe side, he should be castrated anyway.
—HUNTER S. THOMPSON

✦✦

He was a bit like a corkscrew. Twisted, cold, and
sharp.
—KATE CRUISE O'BRIEN

✦✦✦

He's a wit with dunces, and a dunce with wits.
—ALEXANDER POPE

✦✦

Catfight

↔ **Tom Wolfe, according to John Irving**

You see people reading him on airplanes, the same people who are reading John Grisham, for Christ's sake . . . I'm using the argument against him that he can't write, that his sentences are bad, that it makes you wince. You know, if you were a good skater, could you watch someone just fall down all the time? Could you do that? I can't do that.

↔ **Tom Wolfe, according to Norman Mailer**

At certain points, reading [*A Man in Full*] can even be said to resemble the act of making love to a three-hundred-pound woman. Once she gets on top, it's over. Fall in love, or be asphyxiated.

↔ **Tom Wolfe, according to John Updike**

A Man in Full still amounts to entertainment, not literature, even literature in a modest aspirant form. Like a movie desperate to recoup its bankers' investment, the novel tries too hard to please us.

↔ **John Irving, Norman Mailer, and John Updike, according to Tom Wolfe**

Larry, Curly, and Moe. Updike, Mailer, and Irving. My three stooges. . . . *A Man in Full* had frightened them. They were shaken. It was as simple as that. *A Man in Full* was an example . . . of the likely new direction: the intensely realistic novel . . . a revolution in content rather than form . . . that was about to sweep the arts in America, a revolution that would soon make many prestigious artists, such as our three old novelists, appear effete and irrelevant.

Catfight

↪ I wouldn't piss on her if she was on fire.
—Betty Davis on Joan Crawford

↪ Take away the pop eyes, the cigarette, and those funny clipped words, and what have you got? She's phony, but I guess the public likes that.
—Joan Crawford on Bette Davis

↪ The best time I ever had with Joan Crawford was when I pushed her down the stairs in *Whatever Happened to Baby Jane?* —Bette Davis

↪ Why am I so good at playing bitches? I think it's because I'm not a bitch. Maybe that's why Miss Crawford always plays ladies. —Bette Davis

↪ I didn't know her well, but after watching her in action I didn't want to know her well.
—Joan Crawford on Bette Davis

↪ There goes the famous good time that was had by all. —Bette Davis on Joan Crawford

↪ Miss Davis was always partial to covering up her face in motion pictures. She called it "art."

Others might call it camouflage—a cover-up for the absence of any real beauty. —Joan Crawford

Love your enemies . . . it pisses them off.

♦♦♦

Family and Friends

Shotgun wedding—No worries. As long as I can throw my Best Man in front of me, I'm good to go.

♦♦♦

Gotta teach 'em about the birds and the bees—Huh. Even though they've been watching people do it on Cinemax for years, you're still sticking to the whole nature analogy?

♦♦

An apple never falls far from the tree—And isn't it amazing how many bad apples one tree can produce?

♦♦♦

Children should be seen and not heard—Have you seen what some of these kids are wearing? I'll pass on the seeing if you don't mind.

♦♦

Chip off the old block—And still dumber than a rock.

♦♦♦

Any friend of his is a friend of mine—This is the friend that likes to lend people money, right?

++

It's like my daddy used to say—You mean, other than "Don't make me get up or else . . . Shut up and go to bed . . . I'll give you something to cry about . . . Shut up and deal?"

+++

Every parent's worst nightmare—They never have a clue. Their worst nightmare is not even close to how bad it could be.

++

Spare the rod, spoil the child—Use the rod, get six months probation, and you're visiting your child under strict supervision.

+++

Banding together to beat the odds

✦

What's a little

———————

amongst friends

✦

Under the same roof

✦

Some of my best friends

✦

Traditional family values

✦

Creature comforts

✦

A guiding light

✦

A winning combination

✦

Everyman

✦

Hold down the fort

✦

Women and children first!

✦

Welcome to . . .

✦

What began as . . . turned into . . .

✦

They are (he/she is) not alone.

✦

School's out

✦

Motherhood and apple pie—It's getting harder and harder to find authentic versions of either.

✦✦✦

Friendship, *n.* A ship big enough to carry two in fair weather, but only one in foul.
—AMBROSE BIERCE

◆◆◆

~◆~

Three guys go to a ski lodge, and there aren't enough rooms, so they have to share a bed. In the middle of the night, the guy on the right wakes up and says, "I had this wild, vivid dream of getting a hand job!"
The guy on the left wakes up and, unbelievably, he's had the same dream, too.
Then the guy in the middle wakes up and says, "Weird, I dreamed I was skiing!"

~◆~

My mom wanted to know why I never get home for the holidays. I said, "Because I can't get Delta to wait in the yard while I run in."
—MARGARET SMITH

◆◆

I'm still keeping my New Year's resolutions. I only make one because it's the only one easy to keep; I resolve to spend less time with my family.
—MARIA MENOZZI

+++

My father was so cheap that one year he told us Santa didn't come because he wears red and we lived in a Crips zone.
—A. J. JAMAL

++

I'll bet your father spent the first year of your life throwing rocks at the stork.

+++

Yeah, we're friends. Like Hitler and Mussolini.

++

Signs Your Family Is Stressed

1. Conversations begin with "Put down the gun and we can talk."

2. People have trouble understanding your kids because they talk through clenched teeth.

3. No one has time to wait for microwave TV dinners.

4. Family meetings are mediated by law enforcement.

5. You are trying to get your four-year-old to switch to decaf.

My mother used to say that there are no strangers, only friends you haven't met yet. She's now in a maximum security twilight home in Australia.
—DAME EDNA EVERAGE

✦✦✦

I'm a mother with two small children, so I don't take as much crap as I used to.
—PAMELA ANDERSON

✦✦

Snarky Toasts

- ↔ To marriage . . . the rest period between romance.

- ↔ To marriage . . . to some a small word, to others a long sentence.

- ↔ A wedding ring is like a tourniquet; it cuts off circulation.

- ↔ Without marriage, men and women would have to fight with total strangers.

- ↔ May all your ups and downs be between the sheets.

- ↔ Always talk to your wife during lovemaking . . . if there's a phone handy.

- ↔ To our wives and lovers . . . may they never meet.

- ↔ May bad fortune follow you all the days of your life . . . and never catch up to you.

- ↔ To birthdays . . . not so bad considering the alternative.

- ↔ To friends . . . and the strength to put up with them.

Worst Parenting Books of All Time

Last Child in the Woods: Outrunning a Bear

Secrets of the Baby Whisperer: Teaching Your Child to Say, "Huh, What's That Again?"

Our Babies, Ourselves: But Mostly, Ourselves

Confessions of a Slacker Mom: A Lesson in Three Pages

Fatherhood: On Twenty Minutes a Week

My mother had morning sickness after I was born.
—RODNEY DANGERFIELD
✦✦

My mom was a ventriloquist and she always was throwing her voice. For ten years I thought the dog was telling me to kill my father.
—WENDY LIEBMAN
✦✦✦

Good moms let you lick the beaters . . . great moms turn them off first.
—ANONYMOUS
✦✦

You know, Moe, my mom once said something that
really stuck with me. She said, "Homer, you're a big
disappointment," and God bless her soul,
she was really onto something.
—HOMER SIMPSON, *THE SIMPSONS*

✦✦✦

When my husband comes home, if the kids are still
alive, I figure I've done my job.
—ROSEANNE BARR

✦✦

My mother wasn't the protective type. When my
father left, she told us kids, "Don't think this just had
to do with me. Your father left all of us."
—CAROLINE RHEA

✦✦✦

I love my husband, I love my children . . . but I want
something more. Like a life.
—ROSEANNE BARR

✦✦

Top 10 Things Mothers Are Responsible For:[11]

1. Cooking

2. Cleaning

3. Discipline

4. Homework

5. Shopping

6. Transportation

7. Playdates

8. Scheduling

9. Holidays

10. Finding Peace in the Middle East

---

[11] Compare with page 95.

I have good kids. I'm trying to bring them up the right way, not spanking them. I find waving the gun around gets the same job done.
—DENIS LEARY

✦✦✦

You wake up one day and say, "I don't think I ever need to sleep or have sex again." Congratulations, you're ready to have children.
—RAY ROMANO

✦✦

More of the Worst Parenting Books of All Time

Siblings Without Rivalry: Keeping Separate Households in Different States

The Happiest Toddler on the Block: The Joys of Ritalin

The No-Cry Sleep Solution by Jack Daniels

The Baby Bond: 50 Shades of Spit-Up

A father is a man who carries pictures where his
money used to be.
—ANONYMOUS

+++

My father carries around the picture of the kid that
came with the wallet.
—RODNEY DANGERFIELD

++

My father confused me. From the ages of one to
seven, I thought my name was Jesus Christ!
—BILL COSBY

+++

My father only hit me once—but he used a Volvo.
—BOB MONKHOUSE

++

Top 10 Things Fathers Are Responsible For:

1. Sports

2. Teaching them how to defend themselves

3. Movies

4. Beer (to relax from all the work it took for 1–3)

5. See Mom's list

6. See Mom's list

7. See Mom's list

8. See Mom's list

9. See Mom's list

10. See Mom's list

When you're young, you think your dad is Superman. When you grow up, you realize he's just a guy who wears a cape.
—DAVE ATTELL

+++

It is amazing how quickly the kids learn to drive a car, yet are unable to understand the lawnmower, snow blower, or vacuum cleaner.
—BEN BERGOR

++

I've noticed that one thing about parents is that no matter what stage your child is in, the parents who have older children always tell you the next stage is worse.
—DAVE BARRY

+++

Most children threaten at times to run away from home. This is the only thing that keeps some parents going.
—PHYLLIS DILLER

++

Top 10 Lies Children Tell Their Parents:

1. I didn't do it.

2. I didn't do it.

3. I didn't do it.

4. I didn't do it.

5. He/She did it.

6. I didn't do it.

7. I didn't do it.

8. I didn't do it.

9. I didn't do it.

10. I really didn't do it.

~✦~
I asked my husband if he wanted to be in the same room with me when I gave birth. He said, "It would have to be a big room, and there would have to be a bar at one end."
~✦~

In America there are two classes of travel:
first class, and with children.
—ROBERT BENCHLEY

✦✦

They say genes skip generations. Maybe that's why
grandparents find their grandchildren so likeable.
—JOAN McINTOSH

✦✦✦

The best babysitters, of course, are the baby's
grandparents. You feel completely comfortable
entrusting your baby to them for long periods, which
is why most grandparents flee to Florida.
—DAVE BARRY

✦✦

Top 10 Lies Parents Tell Their Children:

1. Eat your vegetables and you'll grow up big and strong.

2. If you're not good, I'm calling Santa.

3. It's a grown-up haircut.

4. It tastes like chicken.

5. All the kids are wearing them.

6. Your teacher called and said you have to spend more time on your homework.

7. After a while, nobody will even notice your braces

8. It's not about winning, it's about going out and having fun.

9. Someday you'll thank me.

10. You're not fat.

Match Game:[12]

Match the saying with who is most likely to have said it.
PARENT OR GRANDPARENT

~•~

1. It's okay, it was old. My mother gave it to me before she died. I didn't need it anymore.

2. You look thin. Can I get you some ice cream?

3. Your father repeated second grade, too.

4. If you don't like what's on your plate, I can make you something else.

5. Go get my wallet; I have a surprise for you.

6. The tooth fairy stopped here as well. He left you ten dollars.

7. Turn the channel, I wasn't watching that anyway.

8. I'm planning on giving you the car when you're ready to drive.

9. I just filled all the candy jars. Help yourself.

10. If you stay over, we can spend tomorrow at the arcade.

I just saw my grandmother, probably for the last time.
She's not sick or anything, she just bores the hell out
of me.
—A. WHITNEY BROWN

✦✦✦

My Nana, ninety years old and still driving . . . not
with me, that would be stupid.
—TIM ALLEN

✦✦

---

12 All are from the grandparent. The parent doesn't say anything, just shakes his or her head in disbelief.

First 10 Years of Anniversary Gifts:

1. Paper

    What That Means To Her: Gift Certificate for spa treatments

    What That Means To Him: Paper for her printer

2. Cotton

    What That Means To Her: 410 Thread Count 100 Percent Egyptian cotton bedsheets

    What That Means To Him: Panties from Wal-Mart

3. Leather

    What That Means To Her: Henri Bendel Alligator satchel

    What That Means To Him: Red faux leather wallet from the Walgreen's rack

4. Flowers

    What That Means To Her: Bouquet of long-stemmed American Beauty roses

    What That Means To Him: Flowers from the produce department of the IGA

    (Have to stop to pick up beer anyway.)

5. Wood

    What That Means To Her: Antique Cherry wood vanity

What That Means To Him: Well, "wood," especially when she wears that hot little pink teddy

6. Candy   What That Means To Her: Belgium chocolate

What That Means To Him: Whitman Sampler

7. Wool   What That Means To Her: Cashmere

What That Means To Him: Hunting socks

8. Linens   What That Means To Her: Lace tablecloth with matching napkins and table runner

What That Means To Him: Absolutely nothing

9. Pottery   What That Means To Her: An antique Chinese tea set

What That Means To Him: A bong

10. Diamond   What That Means To Her: You know

What That Means To Him: Baseball tickets

Family: A social unit where the father is concerned with parking space, the children with outer space, and the mother with closet space.
—EVAN ESAR

✦✦✦

~✦~

An elderly couple was celebrating their fiftieth anniversary at a dinner party. The husband stood up and started telling the story of his dating habits in his youth. It seemed that every time he brought home a girl to meet his mother, his mother didn't like her. So, finally, he started searching until he found a girl who not only looked like his mother and acted like his mother, she even sounded like his mother. So he brought her home one night to have dinner . . . his father hated her.

~✦~

The Law: Politics & Government

Great Moments in Clichés - Presidents

"That government is best which governs the least, because its people discipline themselves."

—Thomas Jefferson

"All right" or "O.K."

—Martin Van Buren

"With me it is exceptionally true that the Presidency is no bed of roses."

—James K. Polk (originated in a Christopher Marlowe poem, but not in the vain we use most today)

"Good ballplayers make good citizens."

—Chester A. Arthur

"Speak softly and carry a big stick."

—Theodore Roosevelt

Great Moments in Clichés - Presidents Redux

"You can fool all of the people some of the time, and some of the people all of the time, but you can not fool all of the people all of the time."

—Abraham Lincoln[13]

"Do I not destroy my enemies when I make them my friends?"

—Abraham Lincoln

"Above all, tell the truth."

—Grover Cleveland

"A man is known by the company he keeps, and also by the company from which he is kept out."

—Grover Cleveland

"And so my fellow Americans, ask not what your country can do for you; ask what you can do for your country."

—John F. Kennedy

---

[13] Before the whole zombie/vampire thing.

Pinko—Used to be a communist sympathizer, today it describes half of the Democrat politicians. Or really cute sweatpants.

✦✦✦

It's harder for a rich man to go to heaven than for a camel to go through the eye of a needle—The only teaching from the Bible that's completely ignored by Republicans.

✦✦

Great Moments in Clichés – Presidents Redux

"A man who has never lost himself in a cause bigger than himself has missed one of life's mountaintop experiences. Only in losing himself does he find himself."

—Richard Nixon

"The time comes upon every public man when it is best for him to keep his lips closed."

—Abraham Lincoln

"Read my lips. No new taxes."

—George H. W. Bush

"The ballot is stronger than the bullet."

—Abraham Lincoln

"I did not have sexual relations with that woman."

—Bill Clinton

"If I had eight hours to chop down a tree, I'd spend six hours sharpening my ax."

—Abraham Lincoln[14]

---

14 (I'm thinking "work smarter not harder.")

"If you can't convince them, confuse them."

—Harry S. Truman

"A friend is one who has the same enemies as you have"

—Abraham Lincoln

When it comes to facing up to serious problems, each candidate will pledge to appoint a committee. And what is a committee? A group of the unwilling, picked from the unfit, to do the unnecessary. But it all sounds great in a campaign speech.
—RICHARD LONG HARKNESS
+++

I honestly believe there are people so excited over this election that they must think that the president has something to do with running this country.
—WILL ROGERS
++

Giving money and power to government is like giving whiskey and car keys to teenage boys.
—P. J. O'ROURKE
+++

Donkey vs. Elephant[15]

A. Bob Hope
[on Lyndon Johnson]
B. H. L. Mencken
[on Franklin D. Roosevelt]
C. Clarence Darrow
[on J. Edgar Hoover]

D. Theodore Roosevelt
[on Woodrow Wilson]
E. U. S. Grant
[on James Garfield]
F. Harry Truman
[on Franklin Pierce]

~ ◆ ~

1. If elected, he will do one thing that is almost incomprehensible to the human mind; he will make a great man out of Coolidge.

2. You can tell he used to be a rancher—he squeezes Republicans like he's milking cows.

3. He is not possessed of the backbone of an angle-worm.

4. If he became convinced tomorrow that coming out for cannibalism would get him votes he needs, he would begin fattening a missionary in the White House backyard.

5. A complete fizzle . . . he didn't know what was going on, and even if he had, he wouldn't have known what to do about it.

6. An infernal skunk in the White House.

As usual, the Liberals offer a mixture of sound and original ideas. Unfortunately none of the sound ideas are original and none of the original ideas are sound.
—HAROLD MACMILLAN

⧫⧫

Conservative, n: A statesman who is enamored of existing evils, as distinguished from the Liberal who wishes to replace them with others.
—AMBROSE BIERCE

⧫⧫⧫

A conservative is a man with two perfectly good legs who, however, has never learned how to walk forward.
—FRANKLIN D. ROOSEVELT

⧫⧫

---

[15] 1.C., 2.A., 3.E., 4.B., 5.F., 6.D.

My kid is a conservative. Why is that? Remember in the '60s, when we told you if you kept doing drugs your kids would be mutants?
—MORT SAHL

+++

We'd all like to vote for the best man, but he's never a candidate.
—KIN HUBBARD

++

I think it's about time we voted for senators with breasts. After all, we've been voting for boobs long enough.
—CLARIE SARGENT

~+~

Bart Simpson: "Didn't you wonder why you were getting checks for doing absolutely nothing?"
Grampa Simpson: "I figured because the Democrats were in power again."

~+~

TOP POLITICAL SLOGANS

1. Reagan—"Are you better off than you were four years ago?"—Huh. And what's the definition of "better off"?

2. Obama—"Yes We Can!"—Well, clearly, no, we can't . . . or better yet, "No, We Don't Wanna."

3. Perot—"Ross For Boss"—What the hell were they thinking?

4. Nixon—"Nixon's The One"—As in, "One, two, test, test . . . is this thing on?"

5. Hoover—"A chicken in every pot and a car in every garage"—The granddaddy of 'em all. Today, no one can afford chicken and there's pot in every garage.

6. Harrison—"Tippecanoe and Tyler Too"—No new ideas? Rhyme something.

7. Eisenhower—"I Like Ike"—See above.

A Higher Power

- ↳ Although He's regularly asked to do so, God does not take sides in American politics.

- ↳ If God had meant for us to vote, he would have given us candidates.[16]

- ↳ If God had been a Liberal, we wouldn't have the Ten Commandments, we'd have the Ten Suggestions.[17]

- ↳ Asked if he prayed for the senators when he served as the Senate chaplain, Edward Everett Hale replied, " No. I look at the senators and pray for the country."

- ↳ Why did God create Democrats? To make used car salesmen look good.

- ↳ Why did God create Republicans? To make used car salesmen look good.

---

[16] Ice-T
[17] Malcom Bradbury

Ann Richards on How to Be a Good Republican:

1. You have to believe that the nation's current eight-year prosperity was due to the work of Ronald Reagan and George Bush, but yesterday's gasoline prices are all Clinton's fault.

2. You have to believe that those privileged from birth achieve success all on their own.

3. You have to be against all government programs, but expect Social Security checks on time.

People want to say there isn't racial profiling at the airport, but let's be honest. If your first name is Mohammed, and your last name isn't Ali, leave a little extra time.
—JAY LENO
+++

How the US Government Does Business Today

A small town in the United States and the place looks almost totally deserted. It is tough times, everybody is in debt, and everybody lives on credit. Suddenly, a rich tourist comes to town. He enters the town's only hotel, lays $100 on the reception counter as a deposit, and goes to inspect the rooms upstairs to pick one. What happens?

1. The hotel proprietor takes the money and runs to pay his debt to the butcher.

2. The butcher takes the money and runs to pay his debt to the pig farmer.

3. The pig farmer pays the supplier of his feed and fuel.

4. The supplier of feed and fuel pay off his escort fees.

5. The escort service pays the hotel for the rooms she rented for clients.

6. The hotel proprietor puts the money back on the counter so that the rich tourist will not suspect anything.

At that moment, the tourist comes down after inspecting the rooms and takes back his money, saying that he did not like any of the rooms. He leaves town.

No one earned anything . . . However, the whole town is now without debt and looks to the future with a lot of optimism.

A Homeland Security official was arrested for soliciting sex from a teenager, who was actually a cop on the Internet. Some of their chats went on for hours, because you know Homeland Security, they take forever to come.

—BILL MAHER

✦✦

REPUBLICANS

It ain't easy bein' a Republican . . . Being a Republican means it's all right to be a bully. After all, God is on your side. Republicans are always right about everything: pro-religion, anti-bureaucracy, pro-military, and pro-business. It's their way or the highway (a highway built with American ingenuity, they would add). At the heart of it all? Money. The gathering and keeping of, hereto with . . . It's enough to make you want to . . . well, snark.

What is conservatism? Is it not the adherence to the old and tried against the new and untried?

—ABRAHAM LINCOLN

An honest politician is one who, when he is bought, will stay bought.

—SIMON CAMERON

Latinos for Republicans. It's like roaches for Raid.
—JOHN LEGUIZAMO

Oh no! The dead have risen and they're voting Republican!
—LISA SIMPSON, *THE SIMPSONS*

GOP: Greed, Oppression, Propaganda.

He's not a Republican, he's a Republican't.

✦

Power corrupts, and absolute power is kinda neat.

✦

Under Republicans, man exploits man. Under Democrats, it's exactly the opposite.

✦

Republicans are so empty headed, they wouldn't make a good landfill.
—JIM HIGHTOWER

✦

Vote Republican. It's much easier than thinking.

✦

A conservative is one who admires radicals centuries after they're dead.
—LEO ROSTEN

✦

I'm not a Republican because I don't make enough money to be that big an asshole.

—PAULA POUNDSTONE

✦

The Republicans' health care plan consists of "'Just say no' to sickness."
—KEVIN POLLACK

✦

Bomb Texas. They have oil!

A POLITICIAN IS . . .

. . . a fellow who will lay down your life for his country.
—TEXAS GUINAN

+++

. . . like quicksilver: if you try to put your finger on
him, you find nothing under it.
—AUSTIN O'MALLEY

++

. . . a person who approaches every subject with an
open mouth.
—ADLAI STEVENSON

+++

. . . a man who can be verbose in fewer words than
anybody else.
—PETER DE VRIES

++

. . . a biped; but he is probably an aberrant form of
hyena.
—ABRAHAM MILLER

Blame the Government for . . .

↔ The financial crisis

↔ Rude department store/DMV/Post Office/ Starbucks employees

↔ People who don't clean up after their dogs

↔ Tailgaters

↔ Spam

↔ Oil spills

↔ Our celebrity-obsessed culture[18]

↔ Never-ending television ads

↔ Pay toilets

↔ The military industrial complex

↔ Fat people stuffing their faces at McDonalds'

↔ Junk mail

↔ The bank bailout

[18] Actually, make that everything bad about the culture.

DEMOCRATS

It ain't easy bein' a Democrat . . . reaching out blindly, knowing what you want but not how to get it . . . that's a Democrat. Being a Democrat means you're only ever so slightly to the right of being a Liberal. You think the Bill of Rights might be "a little outdated." You smoked pot once, in college, and may have inhaled but "don't really remember, it was all a blur." You love NPR and PBS. You "really miss" the '60s, even if you were born ten years after they were over. At the heart of it, Democrats are mostly just easy targets. Observe.

I am not a member of any organized political party. I am a Democrat.[19]

If you get fifteen democrats in a room, you'll get twenty opinions.[20]

Government stimulates the Democratic party.[21]

Bipartisanship. I'll hug your elephant if you'll kiss my ass.

---

[19] Will Rogers
[20] Patrick Leahy
[21] Rush Limbaugh

I never said all Democrats were saloonkeepers. What I said was that all saloonkeepers are Democrats.[22]

Democrats: Cleaning Up Republican Messes Since 1933

✦

I'd rather go hunting with Cheney, than go driving with Ted Kennedy.

Vote Democrat— it's easier than working!

✦

The media are only as liberal as the conservative businesses that own them.

✦

You have to have been a Republican to know how good it is to be a Democrat.[23]

✦

I'm too poor to vote Republican.

_____

[22] Horace Greeley
[23] Jackie Kennedy

MATCH THE PRESIDENT TO THE INSULT[24]

A. George Bush

B. Jimmy Carter

C. Richard Nixon

D. Theodore Roosevelt

E. Calvin Coolidge

F. George Washington

G. Bill Clinton

H. Dwight Eisenhower

~◆~

1. A sordid, ambitious, vain, arrogant, and vindictive knave. [on General Charles Lee]

2. Calling him shallow is like calling a dwarf short. [on Molly Ivins]

3. I worship the quicksand he walks on. [on Art Buchwald]

4. He looks as though he'd been weaned on a pickle. [on Alice R. Longworth]

5. An old maid with testosterone poisoning. [on Patricia O'Tolle]

6. When he gave a fireside chat, the fire went out. [on Anon]

7. Once he makes up his mind, he's full of indecision. [on Oscar Levant]

8. It's the first time he's ever rejected pussy. [on G. Gordon Liddy, When _____ gave away his cat.]

Don't think of it as "gun control," think of it as "victim disarmament." If we make enough laws, we can all be criminals.

✦✦✦

Illegal aliens have always been a problem in the United States. Ask any Indian.

—ROBERT ORBEN

✦✦

---

[24] 1.F., 2.A., 3.C., 4.E., 5.D., 6.B., 7.H., 8.G.

MATCH THE PRESIDENT TO HIS DESCRIPTION[25]

A. Gerald Ford

B. William Taft

C. William Henry Harrison

D. Herbert Hoover

E. Woodrow Wilson

~✦~

1. A flub-dub with a streak of the second-rate and the common. [Theodore Roosevelt]

2. Our President Imbecile Chief. [Andrew Jackson]

3. The air currents of the world never ventilated his mind. [Walter Page]

4. So dumb, he can't fart and chew gum at the same time. [Lyndon B. Johnson]

5. The man offered me unsolicited advice for six years, all of it bad. [Calvin Coolidge]

---

[25] 1.B., 2.C., 3.E., 4.A., 5.D.

Feeling good about government is like looking on
the bright side of any catastrophe. When you quit
looking on the bright side, the catastrophe is still
there.
—P. J. O'ROURKE

+++

The government is like a baby's alimentary
canal, with a happy appetite at one end and no
responsibility at the other.
—RONALD REAGAN

++

If presidents don't do it to their wives, they do it the
country.
—MEL BROOKS

+++

POLITICS IS . . .

. . . the art of looking for trouble, finding it whether it exists or not, diagnosing it incorrectly, and applying the wrong remedy.
—GROUCHO MARX

◆◆◆

. . . the skilled use of blunt objects.
—LESTER B. PEARSON

◆◆

. . . made up largely of irrelevancies.
—DALTON CAMP

◆◆◆

. . . perhaps the only profession for which no preparation is thought necessary.
—ROBERT LOUIS STEVENSON

◆◆

. . . the art of preventing people from sticking their noses in things that are properly their business.
—PAUL VALERY

◆◆◆

. . . the art of postponing decisions until they are no longer relevant.
—HENRI QUEUILLE

✦✦

. . . supposed to be the second-oldest profession. I have come to realize that it bears a very close resemblance to the first.
—RONALD REAGAN

✦✦✦

. . . is like football; if you see daylight, go through the hole.
—JOHN F. KENNEDY

LIBERALS

It ain't easy bein' a Liberal . . . it's the closest thing the American political system has to sanctioning paranoid schizophrenia. If you're a liberal, you are against capital punishment but firmly believe in a woman's right to choose. You think business is bad but that big government is good. It started out so innocently, mostly used as a term with which one could address a classical education. "Liberal" as in liberty . . . free from constraints of the more rigid aspects of society. Libertine . . . libertarian . . . these monikers invoke a touch of the vitriol when spoken by those of "other" doctrine. But, like most words, it was changed and bastardized and got lost along the way.

Liberals want misery spread equally.

✦

Forget the Flag. Burn a Politician.

✦

A liberal is a man who is always willing to spend somebody else's money.[26]

✦

A liberal is a conservative who hasn't been mugged yet.[27]

✦

Question authority before it questions you!

✦

Annoy a liberal. Work hard and smile.

[26] Carter Glass
[27] Frank Rizzo

I've tried to see it from the liberal point of view, but I can't get my head that far up my ass.

◆

The radical invents the views. When he has worn them out the conservative adopts them.[28]

◆

Grow your own dope! Plant a politician!

◆

A liberal is a conservative who has been arrested.[29]

◆

Want to make liberals angry? Defend the United States.[30]

◆

How do you know a liberal is dead? His heart stops bleeding.

---

28 Mark Twain
29 Tom Wolfe
30 Ann Coulter

On Democracy

Democracy means government by discussion, but it is only effective if you can stop people talking.
—CLEMENT ATLEE

✦✦

Democracy is a process by which the people are free to choose the man who will get all the blame.
—LAURENCE J. PETER

✦✦✦

The best argument against democracy is a five-minute conversation with the average voter.
—WINSTON CHURCHILL

✦✦

I believe democracy is our greatest export. At least until China figures out a way to stamp it out of plastic for three cents a unit.
—STEPHEN COLBERT

✦✦✦

Democracy means simply the bludgeoning of the
people by the people for the people.
—OSCAR WILDE

◆◆

Democracy substitutes election by the incompetent
many for appointment by the corrupt few.
—GEORGE BERNARD SHAW

One way to make sure crime doesn't pay would be
to let the government run it.
—RONALD REAGAN

◆◆◆

Politicians are wedded to the truth, but unlike many
other married couples they sometimes live apart.
—SAKI

◆◆

Name the Politicians Who DIDN'T Father a "Love Child" or Two[31]

A. Grover Cleveland

B. John Edwards

C. Strom Thurmond

D. Ulysses S. Grant

E. Thomas Jefferson

F. Benjamin Franklin

G. Jesse Jackson

H. Franklin D. Roosevelt

~✦~

I'd never run for president. I've thought about it, and the only reason I'm not is that I'm scared no woman would come forward and say she had sex with me.

—GARRY SHANDLING

✦✦✦

In the Clinton administration, we worried the president would open his zipper. In the Bush administration, they worry the president will open his mouth.

—JAMES CARVILLE

✦✦

---

[31] D. (Grant) and H. (Roosevelt). While both had affairs, they must have used protection . . . and we ain't talkin' Secret Service here.

Bill Clinton misunderstood the role of the president, which is to screw the country as a whole, not individually.
—BETSY SUSSKIND

♦♦♦

In government, a "highly placed source" is the person who started the rumor.
—SAM EWING

♦♦

I haven't committed a crime. What I did was fail to comply with the law.
—DAVID DINKINS

♦♦♦

The only power any government has is the power to crack down on criminals. Well, when there aren't enough criminals, one makes them. One declares so many things to be a crime that it becomes impossible for men to live without breaking laws.
—AYN RAND

♦♦

Match the Politician to the Sex Scandal[32]

A. Andrew Jackson

B. Barney Frank

C. Bob Barr

D. Jim McGreevey

E. Charles Robb

F. Robert Packwood

G. Eric Massa

H. Wilbur Mills

~✦~

1. While married—to President Johnson's daughter, no less—this senator received a nude massage from Miss Virginia. Was there a happy ending?

2. This congressman introduced the "Defense of Marriage" act—and was subsequently photographed licking whipped cream off strippers at his inaugural party.

3. His diary of sexual exploits really got this senator in trouble when claims of sexual abuse and assault were leveled at him by ten different women.

4. Married a woman presumed to be divorced . . . who wasn't. Huge scandal that was used against

him in the presidential election . . . some thirty years later.

5. Discovered drunk and beaten up, in the company of an Argentinian stripper, with whom he was having an affair.

6. Appointed his male lover to a position in Home-land Security position. His wife wasn't happy.

7. Who said "groping and tickling" weren't just part of a fun work environment? Employees of this congressman.

8. This esteemed congressman had an affair early in his career with a male prostitute who proceeded to service tricks out of his home.

---

[32] 1.E., 2. C, 3, E, 4. A., 5. H., 6. D., 7. G, 8.,B.

Match the Senator to His Sex Scandal[33]

A. Mark Sanford   D. David Vitter
B. John Edwards   E. Gary Hart
C. Larry Craig   F. John Ensign

~✦~

1. He disappeared after telling his wife he was hiking the Appalachian Trail—which turned out to be another woman in Buenos Ares.

2. Had an affair with a staffer (whose husband also worked for him) that was disclosed at his own Fox News press conference.

3. Ran on a big moral platform until he was caught with a high-priced call girl.

4. Arrested at the Minneapolis airport for disorderly conduct after playing footsie with another man in an adjoining men's room stall . . . who turned out to be an undercover agent.

5. Once a VP hopeful, he fell for a filmmaker who he hired to cover his campaign, fathered her child, and used campaign funds to hide it all. The trifecta.

6. "Monkey Business." You remember, the boat, the candidate, the not-his-wife on his lap. 'Nuff said.

A good politician is quite as unthinkable as an honest burglar.
—H. L. MENCKEN

♦♦♦

In a closed society where everybody's guilty, the only crime is getting caught. In a world of thieves, the only final sin is stupidity.
—HUNTER S. THOMPSON

♦♦

---

33 1.A.,2.F.,3. D.,4. C, 5. B., 6. E.

CONSERVATIVES

It ain't easy bein' a Conservative. You have to walk that nearly undetectable line that runs exactly down the middle. You have to maintain the traditional so vehemently that it can make your head spin. And all the while that you're keeping any and all change at the absolute minimum allowable, you are also trying, ever so diligently, to persuade the world that GRADUAL change in society is necessary. Like I said . . . not so easy. Take a look.

Liberals feel unworthy of their possessions. Conservatives feel they deserve everything they've stolen.[34]

✦

A conservative is too cowardly to fight and too fat to run.[35]

✦

A conservative is someone who believes in reform. But not now.[36]

✦

Proud member of the vast right-wing conspiracy

---

[34] Mort Sahl
[35] Elbert Hubbard
[36] Mort Sahl

May the fetus you save be gay

+

Churches should stay out of politics or be taxed.

+

A conservative is a man who just sits and thinks, mostly sits.[37]

+

The Christian Right is neither.[38]

+

Conservatives define them- selves in terms of what they oppose.[39]

Right is right and wrong is wrong, no matter what the spin.

+

Evolution is a theory . . . kind of like gravity

+

I'd rather be waterboarding.[40]

—Conservative bumper sticker

37 Woodrow Wilson
38 Moby
39 George Will
40 Conservative bumper sticker

Organized crime in America takes in over forty billion dollars a year and spends very little on office supplies.
—WOODY ALLEN

♦♦

Nixon told us he was going to take crime out of the streets. He did. He took it into the damn White House.
—RALPH ABERNATHY

♦♦♦

There is no kind of dishonesty into which otherwise good people more easily and frequently fall than that of defrauding the government.
—BENJAMIN FRANKLIN

♦♦

When they call the roll in the Senate, the Senators do not know whether to answer "present" or "not guilty."
—TEDDY ROOSEVELT

♦♦♦

Asking an incumbent member of Congress to vote for term limits is a bit like asking a chicken to vote for Colonel Sanders.
—BOB INGLIS

++

Government is the entertainment division of the military-industrial complex.
—FRANK ZAPPA

+++

Being in politics is like being a football coach. You have to be smart enough to understand the game, and dumb enough to think it's important.
—EUGENE McCARTHY

++

The easiest job in the world has to be coroner. Surgery on dead people. What's the worst thing that could happen? If everything went wrong, maybe you'd get a pulse.
—DENNIS MILLER

+++

CONGRESSIONAL EXCUSES FOR NEVER GETTING ANYTHING DONE

↔ There was massive traffic jam this morning on the way here.

↔ My vote is in the shop.

↔ I couldn't find parking.

↔ I couldn't find my car keys.

↔ I lost my wallet this morning and couldn't leave home without it.

↔ I was mugged coming in today.

↔ I have a doctor's note to leave early that requires me to do less work around here.

↔ I feel ill and should go home early today.

↔ I have [insert disease here] and won't be able to come in to work for a couple of days.

↔ Sorry I'm late . . . I'm moving into a new place.

↔ The power went out last night.

↪ I got food poisoning and won't be able to come in.

↪ What? I didn't know I couldn't do that. Sorry, won't happen again.

↪ I was in the restroom, that's why you couldn't find me. No, not that restroom, the one on the second floor.

↪ I was on a break.

↪ I don't recall that being one of the required skills!

↪ I never got the memo. And [Insert Speaker of House's name] didn't tell me about it.

↪ I really didn't have any clean clothes.

↪ This may sound like a lame excuse, but my dog ate the bill I was working on. No, really, you have to believe me.

↪ [Insert President's name here] told me it was okay to do it.

↪ I was just too drunk to wake up.

If A Cop Pulls You Over . . .[41]

- ➤ Are you Andy or Barney?

- ➤ Don't you know why you pulled me over? Okay, just so one of us does.

- ➤ I thought you had to be in good physical condition to be a police officer.

- ➤ You're not gonna check the trunk, are you?

- ➤ *Obstruction of justice?* No, sir, I prefer to think of it as "avoiding complications."

- ➤ And when the officer says, "Your eyes look red. Have you been drinking?" you probably shouldn't respond with, "Your eyes look glazed. Have you been eating doughnuts?"

---

[41] All of which will get you arrested, beaten, or both—knowing when to snark is a highly desirable quality and skill.

Cop Snark Backatcha

- ➤ Relax; the handcuffs are tight because they're new. They'll stretch out after you wear them a while.

- ➤ Take your hands off the car and I'll make your birth certificate a worthless document.

- ➤ If you run, you'll only go to jail tired.

- ➤ Can you run faster than 1,200 feet per second? In case you didn't know, that is the average speed of a 9mm bullet fired from my gun.

- ➤ So you don't know how fast you were going. I guess that means I can write anything I want on the ticket, huh?

~✦~

A police patrol car was parked outside a bar in Austin, Texas. After last call, the officer noticed a man leaving the bar apparently so intoxicated he could barely walk. The man stumbled around the parking lot for a few minutes, with the officer quietly observing. After what seemed an eternity in which he tried his keys on five different vehicles, the man managed to find his car and fall into it.

He sat there for a few minutes as a number of other patrons left the bar and drove off.

Finally he started the car, switched the wipers on and off—it was a fine, dry summer night—flicked the blinkers on and off a couple of times, honked the horn, and then switched on the lights.

He moved the vehicle forward a few inches, reversed a little, and then remained still for a few more minutes as some more of the other patrons' vehicles left. At last, when his was the only car left in the parking lot, he pulled out and drove slowly down the road. The police officer, having waited patiently all this time, now started up his patrol car, put on the flashing lights, promptly pulled the man over, and administered a Breathalyzer test. To his amazement, the Breathalyzer indicated no evidence that the man had consumed any alcohol at all!

Dumbfounded, the officer said, "I'll have to ask you to accompany me to the police station. This Breathalyzer equipment must be broken."

"I doubt it," said the truly proud redneck. "Tonight I'm the designated decoy."

~✦~

Vice President Dick Cheney accidentally shot a man during a quail hunt . . . making seventy-eight-year-old Harry Whittington the first person shot by a sitting veep since Alexander Hamilton. Hamilton, of course, was shot in a duel with Aaron Burr over issues of honor, integrity, and political maneuvering. Whittington? Mistaken for a bird.
—JON STEWART

✦✦

HarperCollins is paying Scott Brown a lot of money to bare all in his memoirs. What happened to the days when you actually had to do something first to get a book deal? He'll have to wait and read his own book to find out what it is he's actually done.

~✦~

When Dorothy Parker was told that Calvin Coolidge had died, she asked: "How can they tell?"

When he was a young reporter, the journalist Heywood Broun was sent to interview a very stuffy member of Congress on a very controversial subject. "I have nothing to say, young man," said the Congressman haughtily. "I know," said Broun, "now shall we get on with the interview?"

Bessie Braddock to Churchill: "Winston, you're drunk!" Churchill: "Bessie, you're ugly, but tomorrow morning I shall be sober."

~✦~

Match the Insult to the Politician[42]

A. Abraham Lincoln
B. Henry Clay
C. Margaret Thatcher

D. Winston Churchill
E. Henry Kissinger
F. Thomas Jefferson

~♦~

1. They are not fit to manage a whelk stall.

2. Ninety percent of the politicians give the other ten percent a bad name.

3. He is ignorant, passionate, hypocritical, corrupt, and easily swayed by the basest men who surround him.

4. If I could not go to heaven but with a party, I would not go there at all.

5. Whenever I hear anyone arguing for slavery, I feel a strong impulse to see it tried on him personally.

6. In politics if you want anything said, ask a man. If you want anything done, ask a woman.

---

[42] 1. D., 2. E., 3. B., 4. F., 5. A., 6. C.

Winston Churchill

↔ He has all the virtues I dislike and none of the vices I admire.

↔ He's a sheep in sheep's clothing.

↔ He's a modest little person, with much to be modest about.

↔ There but for the grace of God, goes God.

He knows nothing and thinks he knows everything.
That points clearly to a political career.
—GEORGE BERNARD SHAW

✦✦✦

Clinton lied. A man might forget where he parks
or where he lives, but he never forgets oral sex, no
matter how bad it is.
—BARBARA BUSH[43]

✦✦

---

[43] My, oh my, Babs!

I'm like President Ford: I can't do two things at once.
I can't have intercourse and enjoy myself at the same
time.
—RICHARD LEWIS

✦✦✦

When asked if they would like to have sex with me,
30 percent of women said yes, while the other 70
percent replied, "Again?"
—SILVIO BERLUSCONI, ITALIAN PRIME
MINISTER

✦✦

UNITED STATES CAPITOL.

~✦~

President Calvin Coolidge and his wife visited a government farm one day and were taken around on separate tours. Mrs. Coolidge, passing the chicken pens, inquired of the keeper whether the roosters copulated more than once a day. "Yes," the man said. "Dozens of times." "Tell that," Mrs. Coolidge replied, "to the president!" Some time later, the president, passing the same pens, was told about the roosters—and about his wife's remark. "Same hen every time?" he asked. "Oh no, a different one each time," the keeper replied. "Tell that," Coolidge said with a sly nod, "to Mrs. Coolidge."

Several years ago, Reagan, Bush, and Clinton all went on a cruise together. While the ship was out in the sea, it hit an iceberg and started to sink. Quickly, Reagan yelled out, "Women and children first!" Bush then cried, "Screw the women!" To which, Clinton responded, "Do you think we have time?"

~✦~

Oscar is eighty this year, which makes him now automatically the front-runner for the Republican nomination.
—JON STEWART

+++

President Obama held a ceremony at the White House to celebrate the first night of Hanukkah. In response, Republicans said, "It's even worse than we thought. He's a Jewish Muslim."
—CONAN O'BRIEN

++

Work & Money

"Too many people spend money they haven't earned, to buy things they don't want, to impress people they don't like."
—WILL ROGERS

Even money

◆

Filthy rich

◆

Highway robbery

◆

A wheeler dealer

◆

I want my place in the sun

◆

Feather your nest

◆

High and the mighty (the)

◆

Kick butt

◆

Cut a fine figure

◆

Don't use a lot where a little will do

◆

Down the drain/toilet

◆

The fickle finger of fate

◆

Final analysis

◆

Get the sack

◆

Gird your loins

◆

Head honcho

◆

He's a bald faced liar

◆

Reign supreme

◆

Went belly up

All work and no play makes Jack a dull boy—Of course, the same can be said for Bill (Gates), Donald (Trump), and Warren (Buffet)—they all managed "dull" pretty well.

◆◆

She's sleeping her way to the top—Yessir, you talk about your school of hard knocks . . . and nothing but A+ in every class.

◆◆◆

He's had a checkered career—Without the strategic significance a "chess"-ered career might have provided.

◆◆

We're going to burn the midnight oil—It's over there on the shelf next to the daybreak oil, the noontime oil, and the why the hell do I need so many different kinds of "oil" oil.

◆◆◆

Business Clichés

Core Competency—Fundamental strength, although one would think you'd want someone to shoot a tad higher than just "competent."

Buy-In—Agreement on a course of action. Can't just believe, gotta cost ya some jing to boot. Used to a much more useful effect in poker.

Empower—Give added responsibilities to those below you. Can there be anything more condescending? Who are you, the Burger King?

Corporate Values—Corporations are people now? Nope. Soylent green is people, tho.

Make Hay—Be productive or successful quickly. Also used with "while the sun shines" because after the sun goes down, you're going to need to get as soused as you possibly can from all that hay making.

Think Outside the Box—To approach a problem in an unusual way, or using a different method. Overused 101. Every time I hear it, it conjures up those Russian nesting dolls and visions of the speaker stuck inside so many boxes that no one could possibly hear him/her scream.

Leverage—To manipulate or control. As in, to leverage your standing in the community to take unfair advantage over those lesser peons out there.

Vertical—A specific area of expertise. Would really prefer it if you were horizontal, face on the ground.

Learnings—Bizarre conjugations now pass for "expertise." Take the English Language and make it your own. No one will notice.

Boil the Ocean—Waste time. If only you could, we could make the world's largest pot of Moron Soup.

Reach Out—Set up a meeting. I hear that and I want to do a Four Tops pirouette and chime in with "I'll Be There."

Punt—Give up an idea. Also used with "drop back six." Usually said by someone who has blocked more than their share of punts in their day . . . and usually with their face.

Impact—The difference between "affect" and "effect." Your phony affect has had an effect on me—I want to puke.

Give 110 Percent—Can't be done, Sparky. Might be time for that refresher math class . . . from the third grade.

Take It To The Next Level—Make something better. Cool. When you look into your crystal ball and glimpse what that "next level" might be, call me. I'll come a-runnin'.

It Is What It Is—And the World Champion belt and undisputed King of The Obvious crown goes to . . .

Workplace Commentary

➤ This isn't an office; it's hell with fluorescent lighting.

➤ The fact that no one understands you doesn't mean you're an artist.

➤ I have plenty of talent and vision. I just don't care.

➤ I like you. You remind me of when I was young and stupid.

➤ I'm not being rude. You're just insignificant.

➤ I'm already visualizing the duct tape over your mouth.

➤ I will always cherish the initial misconceptions I had about you.

➤ It's a thankless job, but I've got a lot of karma to burn off.

➤ How about never? Is never good for you?

➤ I'm really easy to get along with once you people learn to worship me.

➤ I'll try being nicer if you'll try being smarter.

➤ I might look like I'm doing nothing, but at the cellular level, I'm really quite busy.

➤ I see you've set aside this special time to humiliate yourself in public.

➤ Someday, we'll look back on this, laugh nervously, and change the subject.

➤ If you find it hard to laugh at yourself, I would be happy to do it for you.

➤ Sorry, I can't hear you over the sound of how awesome I am.

➤ I don't work here. I'm a consultant.

➤ How do I set the laser printer to stun?

➤ Who, me? I just wander from room to room.

The Boss

> ➤ I didn't say it was your fault. I said I was going to blame it on you.

> ➤ We passed over a lot of good people to get the ones we hired.

> ➤ My boss said to me, "What you see as a glass ceiling, I see as a protective barrier."

> ➤ He's given automobile accident victims new hope for recovery.

> ➤ He walks, talks, and performs rudimentary tasks, all without the benefit of a spine.

> ➤ To err is human, to blame somebody else shows good management skills.

> ➤ Some people climb the ladder of success. My boss walked under it.

> ➤ My idea of a team effort is a lot of people doing whatever I say.

> ➤ HR manager to job candidate: "I see you've had no computer training. Although that qualifies you for upper management, it means you're under-qualified for our entry-level positions."

Snarky Behavior at Work[44]

➤ When someone asks you to do something, ask if they want that supersized.

➤ Phone someone in the office you barely know, leave your name, and say, "Just called to say I can't talk right now. Bye."

➤ To signal the end of a conversation, clamp your hands over your ears and grimace.

➤ When someone hands you a piece of paper, finger it and whisper huskily, "Mmmmmmm, that feels soooooo good!"

➤ Say to your boss, "I like your style," and shoot him with double-barreled fingers.

➤ Kneel in front of the watercooler and drink directly from the nozzle.

➤ Shout random numbers while someone is counting.

➤ At the end of a meeting, suggest that, for once, it would be nice to conclude with the singing of

---

[44] There is some physical snark involved here. Consult your doctor. Or not.

the national anthem (extra points if you actually launch into it yourself).

➢ After every sentence, say "mon" in a really bad Jamaican accent. As in, "The report's on your desk, mon." Keep this up for one hour.

➢ While a coworker is out, move his or her chair into the elevator.

➢ In a meeting or crowded situation, slap your forehead repeatedly and mutter, "Shut up! Please! All of you just shut up!"

➢ Carry your keyboard over to your colleague and ask if he wants to trade.

➢ Repeat the following conversation ten times to the same person: "Do you hear that?" "What?" "Never mind, it's gone now."

➢ Come to work in army fatigues and when asked why, say, "I can't talk about it."

➢ Posing as a maitre d', call a colleague and tell him he's won a lunch for four at a local restaurant. Let him go.

> ➤ During the course of a meeting, slowly edge your chair toward the door.

> ➤ Arrange toy figures on the table to represent each meeting attendee, and move them according to the movements of their real-life counterparts.

> ➤ Page yourself over the intercom (don't disguise your voice).

> ➤ Encourage your colleagues to join you in a little synchronized chair dancing.

> ➤ Put your garbage can on your desk and label it "in."

> ➤ Reply to everything someone says with, "That's what you think."

> ➤ Finish all your sentences with "in accordance with the prophecy."

> ➤ Send email to the rest of the company to tell them what you're doing. For example: "If anyone needs me, I'll be in the bathroom."

> ➤ Put mosquito netting around your cubicle.

8 Christmas Things Not to Say to Your Boss

1. Did you get anything under the tree?

2. I think your balls are hanging too low.

3. Check out Rudolph's honker!

4. Santa's sack is really bulging.

5. Lift up the skirt so I can get to the bottom.

6. I love licking the end till it's really sharp and pointy.

7. From here, you can't tell if they're real or artificial.

8. To get it to stand up straight, try propping it against the wall.

One Christmas, things were so bad in our house that I asked Santa for a yo-yo and all I got was a piece of string. My father told me it was a yo.
—BRENDAN O'CARROLL

••

AT AN OFFICE PARTY, REMEMBER . . .

- ➤ You are not a stripper.

- ➤ You are not the "life of the party."

- ➤ You are not James Bond.

- ➤ You are not the world's greatest lover.

- ➤ The boss's wife is not hot for you.

- ➤ Suggesting a threesome is not a good idea.

- ➤ It is not cool to drink out of your shoe.

- ➤ Photocopying your buttocks, drilling a hole in the wall to the ladies' room, and shoving crudites into the mail slots will never be funny.

- ➤ Peeing on a computer is a FEDERAL offense.

- ➤ Fashionably late is just late.

- ➤ Your snowman sweater is just dumb, not ironic.

- ➤ Ditto for your reindeer antler headband.

- ➤ Ranting about "The True Meaning of Christmas" could[45] get you beaten up in the parking lot.

---

[45] (and should)

What NOT to Say at Office Xmas Parties

- Man, your wife is smokin' hot—bet you get a ton of UPS deliveries.

- You are so NOT the bitch your husband made you out to be.

- Yes, you're definitely nicer when you're drunk. Maybe you should keep a bottle in your desk?

- Your girlfriend's a really good dancer. Have you gotten her a pole for at home yet?

- No, I'm pretty sure the tinsel would look better on you than the tree.

- I'd love to hear "O Tannenbaum" sung again . . . in German. Reminds me of the rallies in the old country.

- Do your kids ever ask why Santa smells like gin and onion dip?

- I agree. This picture of you and the boss is gonna rock on Facebook.

- Hey, you put a candy cane in a martini and you can barely taste the booze!

➤ You know what would be cool? Taking off our clothes and wrapping ourselves in gift paper. Wanna?

➤ When I screw up at this time of year, I just say, "Santa made me do it!"

Yikes. You moon one person at an office party and suddenly you're not "professional" anymore?
—ANONYMOUS
✦✦✦

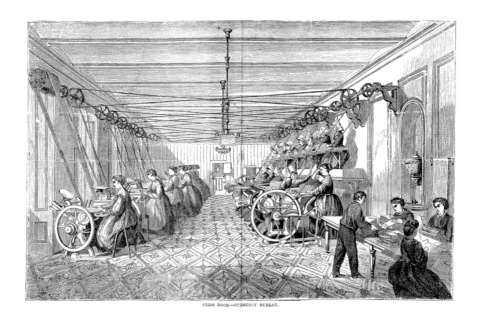

PRESS ROOM—CURRENCY BUREAU.

6 Ways to Drive Your Cube Mate Crazy At Christmastime

1. Wear a Santa suit all the time. Deny you're wearing it.

2. Paint your nose red and wear antlers. Constantly complain about how you never get to join in on the games.

3. Make conversation out of Christmas carols. (E.g., "You know, I saw Mommy kissing Santa Claus underneath the mistletoe last night.")

4. Put on a fake white beard and insist that all your colleagues "give it a yank."

5. Ring jingle bells every fifteen minutes, and say, "Every time a bell rings an angel gets their wings."

6. Steal a life-size nativity scene and display it in your cubicle. When your officemate asks, tell her, "I had to let them stay here, there's no room at the inn."

It's a Job, Okay?

> ➤ There are currently 78 people named S. Claus living in the United States—and one Kriss Kringle.

> ➤ December is the most popular month for nose jobs.

> ➤ Weight of Santa's sleigh loaded with one doll for every kid on Earth: 333,333 tons.

> ➤ Number of reindeer required to pull a 333,333-ton sleigh: 214,206—plus Rudolph.

> ➤ Average wage of a mall Santa: $11 an hour.

> ➤ With real beard: $20.

> ➤ To deliver his gifts in one night, Santa would have to make 822.6 visits per second, sleighing at 3,000 times the speed of sound. At that speed, Santa and his reindeer would burst into flames instantaneously.

> ➤ Of all mall Santa applicants, 7 percent were discovered to have criminal backgrounds.

> ➤ Among Americans, 4 percent believe Santa drives a sports car in the off-season, but 25 percent thinks he drives an SUV.

Snarky Workplace Commentary

↔ Errors have been made. Others will be blamed.

↔ Can I trade this job for what's behind Door One?

↔ Too many freaks, not enough circuses.

↔ Chaos, panic, and disorder—my work here is done.

↔ I thought I wanted a career, turns out I just wanted the paychecks.

↔ Sarcasm is just one more service we offer.

↔ How many people work in your office? About half of them.

↔ Out of my mind. Back in five minutes.

↔ There's too much blood in my caffeine system.

↔ You set low standards and consistently fail to achieve them.

Match the Insult to the Businessman[46]

A. Donald Trump
B. Steve Jobs
C. Henry Ford

D. Bill Gates
E. Ted Turner
F. Warren Buffett

~♦~

1. Be nice to nerds. Chances are you'll end up working for one.

2. Let blockheads read what blockheads wrote.

3. My son is now an "entrepreneur." That's what you're called when you don't have a job.

4. I have made the tough decisions, always with an eye toward the bottom line. Perhaps it's time America was run like a business.

5. Pretty much, Apple and Dell are the only ones in this industry making money. They make it by being Walmart. We make it by innovation.

6. A business that makes nothing but money is a poor business.

---

[46] 1. D., 2. F., 3. E., 4. A., 5. B., 6. C.

Things Not to Say to Your Boss

↔ I wasn't sleeping . . . I was testing my keyboard for drool resistance.

↔ Yes, I can only do one thing at a time. . . . I could do more with a raise, though.

↔ There is nothing left on YouTube to watch!

↔ Hey, I just took this job for the high-speed Internet.

↔ I wasn't daydreaming. Do you discriminate against people who practice yoga?

↔ That's what I like about working for you: total freedom from hero worship. It's refreshing.

↔ I'm not doodling; I thought you were gone for the day.

↔ I have the power to channel my imagination into ever-soaring levels of suspicion and paranoia.

More Snarky Workplace Commentary,

↔ Ah . . . I see the fuck-up fairy has visited us again . . .

↔ I see you've set aside this special time to humiliate yourself in public.

↔ It sounds like English, but I can't understand a word you're saying.

↔ I can see your point, but I still think you're full of shit.

↔ You are validating my inherent mistrust of strangers.

↔ Thank you. We're all refreshed and challenged by your unique point of view.

↔ Yes, I am an agent of Satan, but my duties are largely ceremonial.

↔ No, my powers can only be used for good.

Money, it turned out, was exactly like sex: you thought of nothing else if you didn't have it and thought of other things if you did.

—JAMES BALDWIN

♦♦

Good Life: Food and Drink

No use crying over spilled milk—Milk, no . . . but spill a drop of that single malt scotch, now that's another story.

++

I sleep like a baby—Yeah, well, Percocet and Jamesons will do that for you.

+++

Eat humble pie

Few fries short
of a happy meal

He's a bubble
shy of plumb

**Feast your
eyes on this**

Cut and dried

**He's a corn-fed
hick**

Few sandwiches
short of a picnic

Fat slob

He's an inch
deep and a mile
wide

Get stuffed

Eat dirt

Half seas over

Enough already

He's milktoast

**Hair of the
dog**

Full of himself

Wash your
mouth out with
soap

"They might be dirty, and cheap, and their food might taste like shit, but at least they didn't speak in clichés."
—NEIL GAIMAN

+++

And on the seventh day, God stepped back and said, "This is my creation, perfect in every way . . . oh, dammit I left all this pot all over the place. Now they'll think I want them to smoke it . . . Now I have to create Republicans."
—BILL HICKS

++

The three-martini lunch is the epitome of American efficiency. Where else can you get an earful, a bellyful, and a snootful at the same time?
—GERALD FORD

+++

There is a war on drugs, but I surrendered.
—MARILYN MANSON

++

A man's got to believe in something. I believe I'll have another drink.
—W. C. FIELDS

+++

I even accept for the sake of argument that sexual orgies eliminate social tensions and ought to be encouraged.
—SUPREME COURT JUSTICE ANTONIN SCALIA

++

Now that food has replaced sex in my life, I can't even get into my own pants.

+++

Yeah, I probably shouldn't eat a box of cookies and then puke, but you know what they say: Women who never binge have no souls.

++

~♦~

A drunk walks into a bar, clearly shit-faced. The bartender refuses to serve him. Five minutes later, he comes in again through a side door, but again, the bartender refuses him service. A few minutes later, the drunk comes in the back door, and again, the barkeep refuses to serve him.

"Jesus, man. How many bars do you work at?"

~♦~

The trouble with jogging is that the ice falls out of
your glass.
—MARTIN MULL

◆◆

Back in my drinking days, I would tremble and shake
for hours upon arising. It was the only exercise I got.
—W. C. FIELDS

◆◆◆

Oh, I'm in no condition to drive. Wait a minute.
I don't have to listen to myself. I'm drunk.
—HOMER SIMPSON, *THE SIMPSONS*

◆◆

Warning: Liquor Can . . .

> ➤ Make you believe that ex-lovers are really dying for you to telephone them at four o'clock in the morning.

> ➤ Be a major factor in dancing like an asshole.

> ➤ Cause you to tell the same boring story over and over again until your friends want to smash your head in.

> ➤ Leave you wondering what the hell ever happened to your underwear.

> ➤ Create the illusion that you are tougher, more handsome, and smarter than some really, really, really big biker guy named Bubba.

> ➤ Make you think you are whispering when you are not.

> ➤ Make you think you can seduce members of the opposite sex.

> ➤ Lead you to think people are laughing *with* you.

> ➤ Actually *cause* pregnancy.

In a study, scientists report that drinking beer can be good for the liver. I'm sorry, did I say "scientists"? I meant "Irish people."
—TINA FEY

~✦~

Q: Where does an Irish family go on vacation?
A: A different bar.

~✦~

I'm on a whiskey diet. I've lost three days already.
—TOMMY COOPER

✦✦

I always wake up at the crack of ice.
—JOE E. LEWIS

✦✦✦

If life is a waste of time, and time is a waste of life, then let's all get wasted and have the time of our lives.

✦✦

There's always some amount of gradual, slow burning
destruction over the course of partying.
—GAVIN DEGRAW

✦✦

Partying is such sweet sorrow.
—ROBERT BYRNE

✦✦✦

~✦~

*A drunk phoned the police to report that thieves
had been in his car. "They've stolen the dash-
board, the steering wheel, the brake pedal, even
the accelerator!" he cried out. "Hey, wise guy,"
the cop replied. "Why don't you try getting in the
front seat?"*

~✦~

Reality Check

➢ A bartender is a pharmacist with a limited inventory.

➢ Drugs may lead to nowhere, but at least it's the scenic route.

➢ I'm not addicted to cocaine. I just like the way it smells.

➢ I tried snorting Coke once, but the ice cubes got stuck in my nose.

➢ Time is never wasted when you're wasted all the time.

➢ Rehab is for quitters.

Always do sober what you said you'd do drunk. That will teach you to keep your mouth shut.
—ERNEST HEMINGWAY

✦✦

I'm not a drinker; my body won't tolerate spirits,
really. I had two martinis New Year's Eve and I tried
to hijack an elevator and fly it to Cuba.
—WOODY ALLEN

+++

O God, that men should put an enemy in their
mouths to steal away their brains! that we should,
with joy, pleasance, revel, and applause, transform
ourselves into beasts!
—WILLIAM SHAKESPEARE

++

My grandmother is over eighty and still doesn't need
glasses. Drinks right out of the bottle.
—HENNY YOUNGMAN

+++

I like to keep a bottle of stimulant handy in case I see
a snake, which I also keep handy.
—W. C. FIELDS

+++

The chief reason for drinking is the desire to behave
in a certain way, and to be able to blame it on alcohol.
—MIGNON McLAUGHLIN

++

The harsh, useful things of the world, from pulling
teeth to digging potatoes, are best done by men who
are as starkly sober as so many convicts in the death-
house, but the lovely and useless things, the charming
and exhilarating things, are best done by men with,
as the phrase is, a few sheets in the wind.
—H. L. MENCKEN

+++

First you take a drink, then the drink takes a drink,
then the drink takes you.

—F. SCOTT FITZGERALD

✦✦✦

You've Had Too Much Holiday Cheer When . . .

1. You strike a match and light your nose.

2. A duck quacks—and it's you.

3. You tell your best joke to a plant.

4. The fish bowl looks like a punch bowl.

5. You mistake the closet for a bathroom.

6. When you leave a party, the door locks behind you.

7. You ask for an ice cube and put it in your pocket.

8. While mimicking the biggest bore in the room, you realize it's actually you in the mirror.

CHRISTMAS TOASTS

↔ May your Christmas be full of friends and booze and no socks.

↔ A merry Christmas to all my friends except two or three.

↔ To a fruity, flatulent Christmas!

↔ Merry Stressmas!

↔ Forgive us our Christmases as we forgive them that Christmas against us.

I know a man who gave up smoking, drinking, sex, and rich food. He was healthy right up to the day he killed himself.
—JOHNNY CARSON

✦✦

Media: Movies, Television, and Music

Yellow journalism

✦

Media circus

✦

The liberal media

✦

Sounding off

✦

It sparked a controversy

✦

Case in point

✦

Don't want to cover old ground

✦

Emergency situation

✦

Epidemic proportions

✦

You field this one

✦

Firestorm/storm of protest/ controversy

✦

Go by the book

✦

He's a fall guy

✦

Heated debate

✦

He's an easy study

✦

He's so matter-of-fact

✦

A hidden agenda

✦

I didn't expect the Spanish Inquisition.

✦

I got hosed

✦

Mixed reviews

✦

Nice play, Shakespeare.

✦

Web of intrigue

✦

Tarred and feathered

✦

That's skull duggery

✦

Watch your tongue

✦

An old blowhard

✦

Sworn affidavit

✦

State-of-theart

✦

Great Moments in Clichés — Authors

"Albatross around your neck."

—Samuel Taylor Coleridge

"Our greatest glory is not in never falling but in rising every time we fall."

—Confucius

"The camera makes everyone a tourist in other people's reality, and eventually in one's own."

—Susan Sontag

"It is not only what we do, but also what we do not do, for which we are accountable."

—Moliere

"What's done is done."

—William Shakespeare

"There is no way to prosperity, prosperity is the way."

—Wayne Dyer

"Don't go through life, grow through life."

—Eric Butterworth

"Not all those who wander are lost."

—J. R. R. Tolkien

"Never give in, never give in, never; never; never; never—in nothing, great or small, large or petty—never give in except to convictions of honor and good sense"

—Winston Churchill

"If you don't like something, change it. If you can't change it, change your attitude. Don't complain."

—Maya Angelou

"We are masters of the unsaid words, but slaves of those we let slip out."

—Winston Churchill

Great Moments in Clichés—The Arts

"Eighty percent of success is showing up."

—Woody Allen

"Anything worth doing is worth overdoing."

—Mick Jagger

"Dream as if you'll live forever, live as if you'll die today."

—James Dean

"Success is falling nine times and getting up ten."

—Jon Bon Jovi

"We're born alone, we live alone, we die alone. Only through our love and friendship can we create the illusion for the moment that we're not alone."

—Orson Welles

"You know you are getting old when the candles cost more than the cake."

—Bob Hope

"Truth is like the sun. You can shut it out for a time, but it ain't goin' away."

—Elivs Presley

In every election in American history both parties
have their clichés. The party that has the clichés that
ring true wins.
—NEWT GINGRICH

••

It's a scientific fact. For every year a person lives in
Hollywood, they lose two points of their IQ.
—TRUMAN CAPOTE

•••

Behind the phony tinsel of Hollywood lies the real
tinsel.
—OSCAR LEVANT

••

Great Moments in Clichés—Authors Redux

"A rose by any other name would smell as sweet."

—William Shakespeare

"Don't throw the baby out with the bath water."

—Thomas Murner (loosely credited)

"Bated breath."

—Shakespeare

Best of both worlds—"If this is best of possible worlds . . . all is for the best."

—Voltaire

"The optimist proclaims that we live in the best of all possible worlds; and the pessimist fears this is true."

—James Branch Cable

"Takes the biscuit / Takes the cake."

—James Joyce (in *Dubliners*, 1914, but could have appeared in Latin as early as 1610)

"You can't have your cake and eat it, too."

—John Heywood

"Catch-22."

—Joseph Heller

"A chip off the old block."

—Theocrites, *"A chip of the old flint"*
from the poem "Idylls"

"Cut the mustard."

—O. Henry

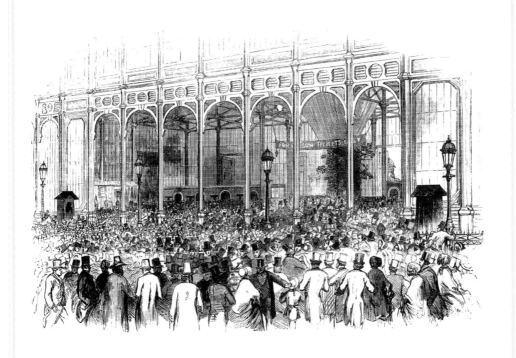

Great Moments in Clichés—The Arts Redux

"In order to succeed, your desire for success should be greater than your fear of failure."

—Bill Cosby

"Just cause you got the monkey off your back doesn't mean the circus has left town."

—George Carlin

"You always pass failure on the way to success."

—Mickey Rooney

"You've achieved success in your field when you don't know whether what you're doing is work or play."

—Warren Beatty

"Behind every successful man is a woman, behind her is his wife."

—Groucho Marx

"Cried all the way to the bank."

—Liberace

Lessons from the Movies

1. It is always possible to park directly outside any building you are visiting.

2. A detective can only solve a case once he has been suspended from duty.

3. Most laptop computers are powerful enough to override the communication systems of any invading alien civilization.

4. It does not matter if you are heavily outnumbered in a fight involving martial arts. Your enemies will wait patiently to attack you one by one by dancing around in a threatening manner until you have knocked out their predecessors.

5. When a person is knocked unconscious by a blow to the head, they will never suffer a concussion or brain damage.

6. No one involved in a car chase, hijacking, explosion, volcanic eruption, or alien invasion will ever go into shock.

7. Any lock can be picked by a credit card or a paper clip in seconds, unless it's the door to a burning building with a child trapped inside.

8. An electric fence powerful enough to kill a dinosaur will cause no lasting damage to an eight-year-old child.

9. Television news bulletins usually contain a story that affects you personally at that precise moment you turn the television on.

10. During all police investigations, it will be necessary to visit a strip club at least once.

11. All telephone numbers in America begin with the digits 555.

12. If being chased through town, you can usually take cover in a passing St. Patrick's Day parade—at any time of the year.

13. All grocery shopping bags contain at least one stick of french bread.

14. Anyone can land a plane, providing there is someone in the control tower to talk him down.

15. Once applied, lipstick will never rub off—even while scuba diving.

16. The ventilation system of any building is the perfect hiding place. No one will ever think of looking for you in there, and you can travel to any other part of the building you want without difficulty.

17. If you need to reload your gun, you will always have more ammunition—even if you haven't been carrying any before now.

18. Talking scarecrows, lions, and great wizards of emerald cities exist, and there is no paperwork involved when your house lands on a witch.

An actor is a guy who, if you ain't talking about him,
he ain't listening.
—MARLON BRANDO

+++

Stephen Spielberg is so powerful he had final cut at
his own circumcision.
—ROBIN WILLIAMS

++

A wide screen just makes a bad film twice as bad.
—SAMUEL GOLDWYN

+++

Yes, I shot a few scenes out of focus. I wanted to win
the foreign film award.
—BILLY WILDER

++

Concession Stand Snark

You're at the concession stand when the two behemoths in the front of the line can't decide between the large popcorn or the super-mega-large popcorn, the ten-pound bag of plain or peanut M&Ms, the gross of Twizzlers, or the garbage pail of Milk Duds. The diet soda is a given. Snark time. Go ahead, let it fly:

➢ "So what? You're feeding an entire African country?"

➢ "How many shows are you staying for?"

➢ "Should I ask the usher for a wheelbarrow?"

➢ "Whatever you do, stay away from the beach, Shamu!"

Snarky Movie Descriptions

➤ *Gone with the Wind*: A movie about a fire, for god's sake.

➤ *Lawrence of Arabia*: Lots of sand, but no selfrespecting gay man would be caught dead wearing what he's got on in most of the movie. Nice uniform, though.

➤ *Casablanca*: A woman walks into a bar. Should be a snark here. There ain't one. And doesn't that piano player know anything else?

➤ *Singin' in the Rain*: An idiot without sense enough to come in out of the rain sings in the rain and nearly drowns.

➤ *West Side Story*: The whitest gangs ever who break into song every time they're supposed to fight.

➤ *Citizen Kane*: Two hours of angst over a sled. A fucking sled.

➤ *On the Waterfront*: Hey pal . . . no way you would been a contender. And leave her goddamn gloves alone.

➤ *The Godfather*: Guy gets pissed. Kills everyone. Even his brother. Kissed him first, though. Nice touch.

➤ *Annie Hall*: La da dee, la di da. Shut the fuck up. Somebody hit her . . . please? And hard. And Grammy Hall while you're at it.

➤ *Star Wars*: Let's see: A woman with two sticky buns on her head, a shag carpet, a vacuum cleaner, and a gay robot save the universe. Could happen.

➤ *The Bicycle Thief*: A kid steals a bike. An old, decrepit, shitty little bike. Yeah, let's go make a movie.

➤ *High Noon*: Three men come into town to kill a sheriff with no facial expressions or any discernible acting ability.

➤ *2001: A Space Odyssey:* In space, no one can hear you yawn. Too bad.

Let the Snark Flow: Small Screen Edition

➤ *Seinfeld/Curb Your Enthusiasm*: Larry David. 'Nuff said?

➤ *30 Rock*: The inimitable Ms. Fey again.

➤ *M*A*S*H*: Great writing and Alan Alda, clearly a Groucho fan.

➤ *The Daily Show*: Meet Jon Stewart, the reigning king of snark.[47]

➤ *The Colbert Report*: Meet Stephen Colbert, the reigning king of snark.[48]

➤ *Californication*: More snark in a half hour than most any other show.

➤ *24*: Guaranteed snark from Chloe to just about everyone.

➤ *SportsNight/West Wing/Studio 60*: Anything from Aaron Sorkin.

---

[47] Or was that Stephen Colbert?
[48] Or was that Jon Stewart?

> *Two and a Half Men*: Even with Charlie Sheen and Jon Cryer, this is a great source.

> *Roseanne*: Made into an art form by Ms. Barr.

> *Rescue Me*: The art form perfected by Denis Leary.

> *House*: Curmudgeons also make for the best snarkers.

> *Arrested Development*: King of the killer asides—the entire show had a snark attitude.

Television is more interesting than people. If it were not, we would have people standing in the corners of our rooms.
—ALAN CORENK

✦✦✦

Television enables you to be entertained in your home by people you wouldn't have in your home.
—DAVID FROST

✦✦

Let the Snark Flow: Literary Edition

- ➤ *The Devil's Dictionary* by Ambrose Bierce

- ➤ *The Portable Dorothy Parker*

- ➤ *Answered Prayers* by Truman Capote

- ➤ Anything on or by Groucho Marx

- ➤ Any of Woody Allen's books

- ➤ *The Portable Juvenal*

- ➤ *The Portable Oscar Wilde*

Imitation is the sincerest form of television.
—FRED ALLEN

✦✦✦

Five Songs Guaranteed to Kill the Mood

1. "Who Let the Dogs Out," Baha Men

2. "Thong Song," Sisqó

3. "Don't Worry, Be Happy," Bobby McFerrin

4. "Smack My Bitch Up," Prodigy

5. "We Are the World," USA for Africa

~•~

Q: What is two hundred feet long and has no pubic hair?
A: The front row at a Jonas Brothers concert.

~•~

Books Every Kid Needs to Read

- *You Were an Accident*
- *You Are Different and That's Bad*
- *The Boy Who Died From Eating All His Vegetables*
- *Fun Four-letter Words to Know and Share*
- *The Kids' Guide to Hitchhiking*
- *Curious George and the High-Voltage Fence*
- *That's It, I'm Putting You Up for Adoption*
- *Grandpa Gets a Casket*
- *Pop! Goes the Hamster . . . and Other Great Microwave Games*
- *Places Where Mommy and Daddy Hide Neat Things*
- *Daddy Drinks Because You Cry*
- *Oh, the Places You'll Scratch and Sniff*
- *Strangers Have the Best Candy*

The Supreme Court says pornography is anything
without artistic merit that causes sexual thoughts;
that's their definition, essentially. No artistic merit,
causes sexual thoughts. Hmm . . . sounds like . . .
every commercial on television, doesn't it?
—BILL HICKS

••

Television: a medium. So called because it is neither
rare nor well done.
—DAVID LETTERMAN

•••

Mozart died too late rather than too soon.
—GLENN GOULD

••

Opera Snark

➤ Opera is when a guy gets stabbed in the back and, instead of bleeding, he sings.

➤ If you throw a violinist and an opera singer off a cliff, which one would hit the ground first? Who cares?

➤ Opera is an experience that starts at six o'clock; after three hours, though, your watch says 6:20.

➤ I liked the opera very much. Everything but the music.

➤ Her singing reminds me of a cart coming down-hill with the brake on.

Snarky Pop Descriptions

➢ He looks like a dwarf who's been dipped in a bucket of pubic hair.[49]

➢ She's about as sexy as a Venetian blind.[50]

➢ I love his work but I couldn't warm to him if I was cremated next to him.[51]

➢ He was a poor black boy who grew up to be a rich white woman.[52]

---

[49] Boy George on Prince
[50] Madonna on Sinead O'Connor
[51] Keith Richards on Chuck Berry
[52] Molly Ivins on Michael Jackson

George Bernard Shaw

↔ I am sorry to have to introduce the subject of Christmas. It's an indecent subject; a cruel, gluttonous subject; a drunken, disorderly subject; a wasteful, disastrous subject; a wicked, cadging, lying, filthy, blasphemous, and demoralizing subject. Christmas is forced on a reluctant and disgusted nation by the shopkeepers and the press: on it's own merits it would wither and shrivel in the fiery breath of universal hatred; and anyone who looked back to it would be turned into a pillar of greasy sausages.

↔ It is really an atrocious institution. We must be gluttonous because it is Christmas. We must be drunken because it is Christmas. . . . We must buy things that nobody wants and give them to people we don't like; because the mass of the population, including the all-powerful middle-class tradesman, depends on a week of license and brigandage, waste and intemperance, to clear off its outstanding liabilities at the end of the year. . . . As for me, I shall fly from it all to-morrow.

↳ Like all intelligent people, I greatly dislike Christmas. It revolts me to see a whole nation refrain from music for weeks together in order that every man may rifle his neighbor's pockets under cover of a ghastly pretence of festivity.

↳ A perpetual holiday is a good working definition of hell.

Match the Criticism to the Book[53]

A. *Paradise Lost*
   (John Milton)
B. *Three Lives*
   (Gertrude Stein)
C. *Moby-Dick*
   (Herman Melville)
D. *Uncle Tom's Cabin*
   (Harriet Beecher
   Stowe)
E. *Franny and Zooey*
   (J. D. Salinger)
F. *A Man in Full*
   (Tom Wolfe)

~♦~

1. Nobody can be more clownish, more clumsy and sententiously in bad taste . . . Oh dear, when the solemn ass brays! brays! brays! —D. H. Lawrence

2. A cold suet-roll of fabulously reptilian length. Cut it at any point, it is the same thing; the same heavy, sticky, opaque mass all through and all along. —Wyndham Lewis

3. The book has gas and runs out of gas, fills up again, goes dry. It is a 742-page work that reads as

if it is fifteen hundred pages long. . . . —Norman Mailer

4. One of the books which the reader admires and lays down, and forgets to take up again. None ever wished it longer than it is. —Samuel Johnson

5. So you're the little woman who wrote the book that made this great war. —Abraham Lincoln

6. It suffers from this terrible sort of metropolitan sentimentality and it's so narcissistic . . . so false, so calculated. Combining the plain man with an absolutely megalomaniac egotism. I simply can't stand it. —Mary McCarthy

---

[53] 1. C., 2. B., 3. F., 4. A., 5. D., 6. E.

Match the Insult to the Book[54]

A. *The Idiot*
   (Fyodor Dostoevsky)

B. *Pride and Prejudice*
   (Jane Austen)

C. *Skinny Bitch*
   (Freedman and
   Barnouin)

D. *Lullaby*
   (Chuck Palahniuk)

E. *Harry Potter and the
   Prisoner of Azkaban*
   (J. K. Rowling)

F. *Fear and Loathing in
   Las Vegas*
   (Hunter Thompson)

~◆~

1. You foul, loathsome, evil little cockroach.

2. You have delighted us long enough.

3. Maybe humans are just the pet alligators that God
   flushed down the toilet.

4. I hate you . . . you are the type, the incarnation, the acme of the most insolent and self-satisfied, the most vulgar and loathsome commonplaceness. Yours is the commonplaceness of pomposity, of self-satisfaction and olympian serenity. You are the most ordinary of the ordinary!

5. Is that a beard, or are you eating a muskrat?

6. Coffee is for pussies.

---

[54] 1. E., 2. B., 3. D., 4. A., 5. F., 6. C.

Oscar Wilde

→ There are two ways of disliking poetry; one way is to dislike it, the other is to read Pope.

→ He has no enemies, but is intensely disliked by his friends.

→ Some cause happiness wherever they go; others whenever they go.

→ Fashion is what one wears oneself. What is unfashionable is what other people wear.

→ When the gods wish to punish us they answer our prayers.

→ I don't recognize you—I've changed a lot.

→ Only dull people are brilliant at breakfast.

→ One should always be in love. This is the reason one should never marry.

→ Fashion is a form of ugliness so intolerable that we have to alter it every six months.

→ She is a peacock in everything but beauty.

↪ He hadn't a single redeeming vice.

↪ He has one of those characteristic British faces that, once seen, are never remembered.

↪ The play was a great success, but the audience was a disaster.

Shakespearean Insults[55]

- ↪ Thou detestable maw, thou womb of death.

- ↪ No longer from head to foot than from hip to hip, she is spherical, like a globe; I could find out countries in her.

- ↪ Thou lump of foul deformity.

- ↪ Thou unfit for any place but hell.

- ↪ He heareth not, he stirreth not, he moveth not, the ape is dead.

- ↪ You kiss by the book.

- ↪ Why, he's a man of wax.

- ↪ You should be women, and yet your beards forbid me to interpret that you are so.

- ↪ Whose horrible image doth unfix my hair and make my seated heart knock at my ribs.

- ↪ What you egg! You fry of treachery!

- ↪ Fit to govern! No, not to live.

↪ I had rather be a toad, and live upon the vapour of a dungeon, than keep a corner in the thing I love for others' uses.

↪ Damn her, lewd minx!

↪ You have such a February face, so full of frost, of storm and cloudiness.

↪ I do not like thy look, I promise thee.

↪ You Banbury cheese!

↪ Thou disease of a friend.

---

55 You may not understand them, but they certainly *sound* insulting.

Match the Insult to the Show[56]

A. *Guys and Dolls*   D. *Gypsy*

B. *Glengarry Glen Ross*   E. *Romeo and Juliet*

C. *West Side Story*   F. *Come Back, Little Sheba*

~✦~

1. Thy head is as full of quarrels as an egg is full of meat.

2. Why don't you get smart, you stupid hooligans? I oughta take you down to the station and throw you in the can right now. You and the tin-horn immigrant scum you come from.

3. I kinda like it when you forget to give me presents. It makes me feel like we're married.

4. You're like a pioneer woman without a frontier.

5. Alcoholics are mostly disappointed men.

6. Cop couldn't find his fucking couch in the living room.

---

[56] 1. E., 2. C., 3. A., 4. D., 5. F., 6. B.

If we were the Monkees, we'd be ready by now.
—FRANK ZAPPA [while band was still tuning
their instruments]

+++

He has Van Gogh's ear for music.
—BILLY WILDER

++

I'd harbored hopes that the intelligence that once
inhabited novels or films would ingest rock. I was
wrong.
—LOU REED

+++

More Shakespearean Insults

- ↬ Your means are very slender, and your waste is great.

- ↬ You are as a candle, the better part burnt out.

- ↬ I think he be transformed into a beast, for I can nowhere find him like a man.

- ↬ Away! Thou art poison to my blood.

- ↬ As I told you always, her beauty and her brain go not together.

- ↬ I'll pray a thousand prayers for thy death.

- ↬ Come, you are a tedious fool.

- ↬ Were I like thee, I would throw away myself.

- ↬ Would thou wert clean enough to spit upon!

- ↬ I'll beat thee, but I should infect my hands.

- ↬ Thou art like the harpy, which, to betray, dost with thine angels face, seize with thine eagle's talons.

↪ Your peevish chastity, which is not worth a breakfast in the cheapest country.

↪ He is open to incontinency.

↪ A knot you are of damned blood-suckers.

↪ Thy mother's name is ominous to children.

↪ Pray you, stand farther from me!

↪ You blocks, you stones, you worse than sense-less things!

↪ There's many a man hath more hair than wit.

↪ If thou art chang'd to aught, tis to an ass.

Match the Insult to the Movie[57]

A. *Christmas Vacation*   D. *Dazed and Confused*
B. *The Ref*   E. *The Departed*
C. *The Big Sleep*   F. *Garden State*

~✦~

1. I'm the guy that does his job. You must be the other guy.

2. My, my, my. So many guns around town and so few brains.

3. What are you looking at? Wipe that face off your head, bitch.

4. Can I refill your eggnog for you? Get you something to eat? Drive you out to the middle of nowhere and leave you for dead?

5. If there was a retarded Oscar you would win, hands down.

6. You know what I'm going to get you next Christmas, Mom? A big wooden cross, so that every time you feel unappreciated for your sacrifices, you can climb on up and nail yourself to it.

---

[57] 1. E., 2. C., 3. D., 4. A., 5. F., 6. B.

Match the Insult to the Sitcom[58]

A. *The Office*
   (Dwight Schrute)

B. *Roseanne*
   (Roseanne)

C. *The Muppet Show*
   (Statler and Waldorf)

D. *Curb Your Enthusiasm*
   (Larry David)

E. *The Simpsons*
   (Groundskeeper Willie)

F. *Family Guy*
   (Stewie Griffin)

~♦~

1. Well, I'd love to stay and chat, but you're a total bitch.

2. Bonjour, you cheese-eating surrender-monkeys!

3. Switzerland is a place where they don't like to fight, so they get people to do their fighting for them while they ski and eat chocolate.

4. Dolphins get a lot of good publicity for the drowning swimmers they push back to shore, but what you don't hear about is the many people they

push farther out to sea! Dolphins aren't smart.
They just like pushing things.

5. Your idea of romance is popping the can away from
my face.

6. Wake up, you old fool, you slept through the show.
Who's a fool? You watched it.

---

[58] 1. F., 2. E., 3. D., 4. A., 5. B., 6. C.

Match the Quote to the Movie: In-Laws Edition[59]

A. *The Proposal*   D. *The In-Laws*

B. *The Princess Bride*   E. *Monster-in-Law*

C. *Meet the Parents*

~•~

1. - I mean, can you ever really trust another human being, Greg?

    - Sure, I think so.

    - No. The answer is you cannot.

2. - [*taking a knitted blanket out of the cabinet*] If you get chilly tonight use this. It has special powers.

    - Oh. What kind of special powers?

    - I call it the baby maker.

    - Okay.

    [*to Andrew*]

    - Better be super careful with this.

3. - I'm sorry I called you the worst father in the world. I'm sure there're at least two or three guys who are worse.

    - Thank you, Jer.

4. - Marriage is a sacred union which must only be entered with the utmost care.

    - Weren't you married four times?

5. - What was that for?

    - Because you have always been so kind to me, and I won't be seeing you again since I'm killing myself once we reach the honeymoon suite.

    - Won't that be nice. She kissed me, ha, ha, ha!

---

[59] 1. C., 2. A., 3. D., 4. E., 5. B.

Match the Quote to the Movie: Father Edition[60]

A. *Fight Club*

B. *Father of the Bride*

C. *Empire Falls*

D. *3 Men and a Baby*

E. *A Chorus Line*

~•~

1. -Drive carefully. And don't forget to fasten your condom.
   -Dad!
   -Seat belt! I meant, I meant seat belt.

2. I couldn't catch a ball if it had Elmer's Glue all over it. And my father had to be this ex-football star. He didn't know what to tell his friends, so he told them all I had polio. On Father's Day, I used to limp for him.

3. All we have to do is feed it, it'll shut up.

4. Shut up! Our fathers were our models for God. If our fathers bailed, what does that tell you about God?

5. To tell you the truth, I would rather have a complete idiot for a child than an ingrate.

Match the Quote to the Movie: Family Edition[61]

A. *Juno*

B. *The Lion King*

C. *Four Christmases*

D. *Groundhog's Day*

E. *Mean Girls*

~◆~

1. - You lie to your family at Christmas time?
    - Well, you can't really spell families with lies . . .

2. It's the same thing your whole life . . . clean up your room, stand up straight, pick up your feet, take it like a man, be nice to your sister, don't mix beer and wine, ever . . . oh yeah, don't drive on the railroad tracks . . .

3. - You should look at adoption ads; I see them all the time in the Penny Saver . . .
    - They have ads for parents?
    - Yeah, desperately seeking spawn, right next to like terriers, and iguanas, and used fitness equipment and stuff.

4. - Where's Cady?

- She went out.

- She's grounded.

- [*surprised*] Are they not suppose to be let out when they're grounded?

5. - Is that a challenge?

- Temper, temper. I wouldn't *dream* of challenging you.

- Pity! Why not?

- Well, as far as brains go, I got the lion's share. But, when it comes to brute strength . . . I'm afraid I'm at the shallow end of the gene pool.

---

[61] 1. C., 2. D., 3. A., 4. E., 5. B.

Match the Quote to the Movie: Siblings Edition[62]

A. *Harry Potter and the Sorcerer's Stone*

B. *The Godfather, Part I*

C. *Home for the Holidays*

D. *The Godfather, Part II*

E. *The Parent Trap*

F. *Chinatown*

~♦~

1. I know it was you. You broke my heart. You broke my heart!

2. Come on, you think I'd make my sister a widow?

3. - She's my daughter. [slap]

   - I said I want the truth!

   - She's my sister . . . [slap] She's my daughter . . .

   - [slap] My sister, my daughter . . .

   - [More slaps] She's my sister *and* my daughter!

4. - You don't know the first thing about me.

    - Likewise, I'm sure. If I just met you on the street
    . . . if you gave me your phone number . . . I'd
    throw it away.

    - Well, we don't have to like each other, Jo. We're
    family.

5. - Fred, you next.

    - He's not Fred, I am!

    - Honestly, woman. You call yourself our mother.

    - [*to Fred*] Oh, I'm sorry, George.

    - I'm only joking, I am Fred!

6. - You wanna know the *real* difference between us?

    - Let me see . . . I know how to fence and you don't
    . . . Or I have class and you don't. Take your pick.

    - Why I oughta!

---

[62] 1. D., 2. B., 3. F., 4. C., 5. A., 6. E.

Match the Quote to the Movie: Children Edition[63]

A. *Hot Fuzz*

B. *Finding Neverland*

C. *Spy Kids*

D. *Up*

E. *Beauty and the Beast*

~✦~

1. -Do you want to play a game? It's called "See Who Can Go the Longest Without Saying Anything."
    -Cool! My mom loves that game!

2. - It's Frank! He's appointed himself Judge, Jury and Executioner.
    - He is not Judge Judy and Executioner!

3. Do I still have to sleep in the cupboard?

4. Our parents can't be spies . . . they're not cool enough!

5. - This is Jack. Second in line to the throne. And that one's Michael. He's only five.
    - And I'm in prison for it.

---

[63] 1. D., 2. A., 3. E., 4. C., 5. B.

Match the Quote to the Movie: Mother Edition[64]

A. *Mamma Mia!*   D. *Wyatt Earp*

B. *Mask*   E. *Psycho*

C. *Step Brothers*

~•~

1. My Mama always said don't put off 'til tomorrow who you can kill today.

2. Somebody up there has got it in for me. I bet it's my mother.

3. I swear, I'm so pissed off at my mom. As soon as she's of age, I'm putting her in a home.

4. A boy's best friend is his mother.

5. First you told me he was gonna be retarded, then you told me he was gonna be blind *and* deaf. If I'd dug his grave every time one of you geniuses told me he was gonna die, I'd be eating chop suey in China by now!

---

[64] 1. D., 2. A., 3. C., 4. E., 5. B.

Match the Quote to the Movie:
Grandparents Edition[65]

A. *Little Miss Sunshine*   C. *The 40-Year-Old Virgin*
B. *The Bucket List*   D. *The Philadelphia Story*

~✦~

1. I would sell my grandmother for a drink—and you know how I love my grandmother.

2. That's a good looking grandma! My grandma looks like Jack Palance.

3. We live, we die, and the wheels on the bus go round and round.

4. - Grandpa, am I pretty?
   - You are the most beautiful girl in the world.
   - You're just saying that.
   - No! I'm madly in love with you and it's not because of your brains or your personality.

---

[65] 1. D., 2. C., 3. B., 4. A.

Chapters in Justin Bieber's New Book

Chapter 6—The Day My Face Broke Out

Chapter 10—My First Wet Dream

Chapter 12—Three Girls at Once

Chapter 14—The Day My Face Broke Out Again

Chapter 20—Learning to Drive

Chapter 21—Learning to Parallel Park

Chapter 22—Tipping My Driver

Chapter 30—Four Girls at Once

Chapter 35—The Day My Voice Changed and
My Career Ended

Dorothy Parker

↔ You can lead a horticulture, but you can't make her think.

↔ His voice was as intimate as the rustle of bed-sheets.

↔ Brevity is the soul of lingerie.

↔ One more drink and I'd be under the host.

↔ Tell him I've been too fucking busy—or vice versa.

↔ Ducking for apples—change one letter and it's the story of my life.

William Shakespeare

↪ Is it not strange that desire should so many years outlive performance?

↪ Were kisses all the joys in bed, One woman would another wed.

↪ All lovers swear more performance than they are able.

↪ Can one desire too much of a good thing?

↪ Drink, sir, is a great provoker of three things . . . nose-painting, sleep, and urine. Lechery, sir, it provokes, and unprovokes; it provokes the desire, but it takes away the performance.

Woody Allen

- Remember, if you smoke after sex, you're doing it too fast.

- If there is reincarnation, I'd like to come back as Warren Beatty's fingertips.

- My brain is my second-favorite organ.

- I'm such a good lover because I practice a lot on my own.

- I was involved in an extremely good example of oral contraception two weeks ago. I asked a girl to go to bed with me, and she said no.

- My wife and I thought we were in love, but it turned out to be benign.

- Sex between a man and a woman can be wonderful, provided you get between the right man and the right woman.

- I sold the memoirs of my sex life to a publisher. They're going to make a board game out of it.

- I think people should mate for life, like pigeons or Catholics.

~+~

Elaine: I've yada yada'd sex.

George: Really?

Elaine: Yeah. I met this lawyer, we went out to dinner, I had the lobster bisque, we went back to my place, yada yada yada, I never heard from him again.

Jerry: But you yada yada'd over the best part.

Elaine: No, I mentioned the bisque.

—SEINFELD

~+~

What Shakespeare Really Meant[66]

↔ Self-love, my liege, is not so vile a sin, as self-neglecting.
Translation: We should masturbate more.

↔ Be to yourself as you would to your friend.
Translation: It's okay to sleep with your sister because your friend sure would.

↔ Have patience, and endure.
Translation: Use one of those numbing creams if you have to. Or try wearing five condoms at once.

↔ They that thrive well take counsel of their friends.
Translation: If your drinking buddies say she's really a man, listen to them.

↔ That man that hath a tongue, I say, is no man, if with his tongue he cannot win a woman.
Translation: If you're desperate to impress her, you can always resort to oral sex.

↪ O, flatter me, for love delights in praises.
Translation: Honesty isn't necessarily the best policy when it comes to penis size.

↪ Praising what is lost, makes the remembrance dear.
Translation: When you're telling your buddies about your conquests, exaggerate. A lot.

↪ My endeavors have ever come too short of my desires.
Translation: You've never had twins and you never will. Get over it.

---

⁶⁶ Reprinted with permission from Scott Roeben.

Mae West

➤ I consider sex a misdemeanor; the more I miss, de meaner I get.

➤ To err is human—but it feels divine.

➤ I feel like a million tonight. But one at a time.

➤ An orgasm a day keeps the doctor away.

➤ I only like two kinds of men—domestic and imported.

➤ Thanks, I enjoyed every inch of it.

➤ I'm single because I was born that way.

➤ When it comes to men, she never turns down anything except the bedcovers.

➤ When women go wrong, men go right after them.

Groucho Marx

> ➤ Whoever called it necking was a poor judge of anatomy.

> ➤ Marry me and I'll never look at another horse!

> ➤ I chased a girl for two years only to discover that her tastes were exactly like mine: we were both crazy about girls.

> ➤ I remember the first time I had sex—I kept the receipt.

> ➤ I was married by a judge . . . I should have asked for a jury.

> ➤ I read so many bad things about sex that I had to give up reading.

Sports

Nothing brings out one's inner snark more than the thrill of victory or the agony of your feet. Or the agony of defeat—I was never quite sure which it was. Anyway, competition breeds contempt and contempt is a gateway drug to snark, so . . . You can't deny you did steroids if your head is wider than it is tall.

—BILL MAHER

Although golf was originally restricted to wealthy, overweight Protestants, today it's open to anybody who owns hideous clothing.

—DAVE BARRY

Sure, there have been injuries and deaths in boxing— but none of them were serious.

—ALAN MINTER

Every day you guys look worse and worse. And today
you played like tomorrow.
—JOHN MARIUCCI

♦♦♦

The only reason I don't like playing in the World
Series is I can't watch myself play.
—REGGIE JACKSON

♦♦

I may be dumb, but I'm not stupid.
—TERRY BRADSHAW

♦♦♦

There's a fine line between fishing and just standing
on the shore like an idiot.
—STEVEN WRIGHT

♦♦

It's good sportsmanship to not pick up lost golf balls
while they are still rolling.
—MARK TWAIN

♦♦♦

The other day I broke 70. That's a lot of clubs.
—HENNY YOUNGMAN

♦♦

Cross-country skiing is great if you live in a small
country.
—STEVEN WRIGHT

♦♦♦

Every time a baseball player grabs his crotch, it makes
him spit. That's why you should never date a baseball
player.
—MARSHA WARFIELD

♦♦

You all act like it's a big deal to gain weight when you
get old. I got it down to an exact science.
—CHARLES BARKLEY *on the Barry Bonds
steroid allegations*

♦♦♦

Sports Clichés Made Irrelevant

➤ If practice makes perfect, and no one is perfect, why practice?

➤ It definitely is winning, not how you play the game, because if you don't win, no one remembers how you played the game, only that you lost, you schmuck.

➤ Pain is only temporary, but victory is forever. (*Uh, no. I still have pain from playing football in high school and, even on a good day, I can't remember who we beat.*)

➤ When you put on that jersey, the name on the front is more important than the name on the back. (*Hey, what happens when you put it on backward?*)

➤ The vision of a champion is someone who is bent over, drenched in sweat, at the point of exhaustion when no one else is watching. (*Sounds more like what happens in the locker room after the game—or in prison.*)

➤ There is no glory in practice, but without practice, there is no glory. (*But, occasionally, there's glory after a little practice and practice with only a little glory . . . or a lot of glory and very little practice . . . or some glory with only a teaspoon of practice . . . and . . . Jesus, why bother?*)

If one synchronized swimmer drowns, do the rest have to drown, too?

◆◆

Skiing, n. The art of catching cold and going broke while rapidly heading nowhere at great personal risk.

~◆~

"Why don't you play golf with Drew anymore?" the wife asked her husband.

"Would you play with someone who moves his ball to a better lie when no one is looking, deliberately coughs through his opponents, backswing, and lies about his handicap?"

"Well, no," said the wife.

"Yeah, well neither will he."

~◆~

I watched the Indy 500, and I was thinking that if
they left earlier they wouldn't have to go so fast.
—STEVEN WRIGHT

++

It's basically the same, just darker.
—ALAN KULWICKI, STOCK CAR RACER
*on racing Saturday nights as opposed to Sunday
afternoons*

+++

All I had to do is keep turning left!
—GEORGE ROBSON, *WINNER OF THE
1946 INDY 500*

++

Booze, broads, and bullshit. If you got all that, what
else do you need?
—HARRY CARAY

+++

From the Mouths of Commentators

➢ The lead car is absolutely, truly unique, except for the one behind it, which is exactly identical to the one in front of the similar one in back.

➢ He dribbles a lot and the opposition doesn't like it. In fact, you can see it all over their faces.

➢ I saw her snatch this morning during her warmup and it was amazing.[67]

➢ This is really a lovely horse and I speak from personal experience since I once mounted her mother.

➢ Julian Dicks is everywhere. It's like they've got eleven Dicks on the field.

➢ One of the reasons Arnie Palmer is playing so well is that before each final round, his wife takes out his balls and kisses them.

---

[67] It's about weight-lifting, you perv. Weight-lifting.

I'm not an athlete. I'm a professional baseball player.
—JOHN KRUK

++

Like they say, it ain't over till the fat guy swings.
—DARREN DAULTON, PHILLIES
CATCHER *on stocky first baseman John Kruk*

+++

I dunno. I never smoked any Astroturf.
—TUG McGRAW *asked whether he preferred grass or AstroTurf*

++

I told [General Manager] Roland Hemond to go
out and get me a big name pitcher. He said, "Dave
Wehrmeister's got eleven letters. Is that a big enough
name for you?"
—EDDIE EICHORN, WHITE SOX OWNER

+++

Raise the urinals.
—DARREL CHANEY *on how management could keep the Braves on their toes*

··

I don't care what the tape says. I didn't say it.
—RAY MALAVASI, FOOTBALL COACH

···

I'm not allowed to comment on lousy officiating.
—JIM FINKS, NEW ORLEANS SAINTS GENERAL MANAGER, *when asked after a loss what he thought of the refs*

··

Better teams win more often than the teams that are not so good.
—TOM WATT, EX-MAPLE LEAFS COACH
(his team was not so good)

···

He's the man of the hour at this particular moment.
—DON KING

++

My handicap is that I don't have a big enough beer
cooler for the back of my golf cart.
—NFL PLAYER *on his golf handicap*

+++

Ninety percent of putts that are short don't go in.
—YOGI BERRA

++

I say to the gun owner who owns an AK-47, if it
takes a hundred rounds to bring down a deer, maybe
hunting isn't your sport.
—ELLEN DEGENERES

+++

For most amateurs, the best wood is in the bag: the pencil.
—CHI CHI RODRIQUEZ

++

I have a tip that can take five strokes off anyone's golf game. It's called an eraser.
—ARNOLD PALMER

+++

I owe a lot to my parents, especially my mother and father.
—GREG NORMAN

++

Match the Insult to the Athlete[68]

A. Muhammed Ali   D. George Best
B. Torii Hunter   E. Maria Sharapova
C. Roy Keane   F. John McEnroe

~✦~

1. You were a crap player, you are a crap manager. The only reason I have any dealings with you is that somehow you are manager of my country and you're not even Irish, you English ****. You can stick it up your bollocks.

2. I'm not the next [Anna] Kournikova—I want to win matches.

3. Joe Frazier is so ugly he should donate his face to the US Bureau of Wildlife.

4. What problems do you have, apart from being unemployed, a moron, and a dork?

5. He cannot kick with his left foot, he cannot head a ball, he cannot tackle, and he doesn't score many goals. Apart from that he's all right.

6. Why should I get this kid from the South Side of Chicago and have Scott Boras represent him and pay him $5 million when you can get a Dominican guy for a bag of chips?

---

[68] 1. C., 2. E., 3. A., 4. F., 5. D., 6. B.

Caddie Snark

Golfer: Any way how I can cut ten strokes off my score?

Caddie: Yes, quit on the seventeenth hole.

Golfer: I'd move Heaven and Earth to break 100 on this course.

Caddie: Try Heaven, you've already moved most of the Earth.

Golfer: Think I'm going to drown myself in the lake.

Caddie: Think you can keep your head down that long?

Golfer: Caddie, how would you have played that last shot?

Caddie: Under an assumed name.

Things in Golf That Sound Dirty

1. After eighteen holes, I can barely walk.

2. You really whacked the hell out of that sucker.

3. Mind if I join your threesome?

4. Keep your head down and spread your legs a bit more.

5. Hold up . . . I need to wash my balls first.

Match the Sex Euphemism to the Sport[69]

A. Soccer
B. Most sports
C. Football
D. Boxing

E. Baseball
F. Basketball
G. Golf
H. Hockey

~♦~

1. Pitcher or catcher?

2. Putting from the rough.

3. Pulling the goalie.

4. Take one for the team.

5. Take it to the hole.

6. Stuffed it in the end zone.

7. Deep in the hole.

8. Hitting the canvas.

---

[69] 1. E, 2. G, 3. H, 4. B, 5. F, 6. C, 7. A, 8. D

It's weird when you watch women's tennis now, with all the grunting and shouting. It's like phone sex. You have to be very careful not to get too excited.
—ROBIN WILLIAMS

++

Hitting is better than sex.
—REGGIE JACKSON

+++

Fifty percent of life in the NBA is sex.
The other 50 percent is money.
—DENNIS RODMAN

++

Sports Clichés That Could Be About Sex

> Practice as if you are the worst; perform as if you are the best.
> —JOHN WOODEN

+++

> It is deceptively simple and endlessly complicated; it satisfies the soul and frustrates the intellect. It is at the same time rewarding and maddening—and it is, without a doubt, the greatest game mankind has ever invented.
> —ARNOLD PALMER

++

> It has nothing to do with fair play. It is bound up with hatred, jealousy, boastfulness, disregard of all rules, and sadistic pleasure in witnessing violence. In other words, it is war minus the shooting.
> —GEORGE ORWELL

+++

➢ If you aren't playing well, it isn't as much fun. When that happens, I tell myself just to go out and play as I did when I was a kid.
—THOMAS WATSON

✦✦

➢ We didn't lose the game; we just ran out of time.
—VINCE LOMBARDI

✦✦✦

➢ If everything seems under control, you're just not going fast enough.
—MARIO ANDRETTI

✦✦

➢ If you're not just a little bit nervous before a match,
you probably don't have the expectations of yourself
that you should have.
—HALE IRWIN

✦✦✦

➢ Adversity causes some men to break; others to
break records.
—WILLIAM A. WARD

✦✦

➢ Nobody's a natural. You work hard to get good
and then work to get better. It's hard to stay on top.
—PAUL COFFEY

✦✦✦

➤ The biggest things are often the easiest to do
because there is so little competition.
—WILLIAM VAN HORNE

✦✦✦

➤ It breaks your heart. It is designed to break your
heart. The game begins in the spring when everything
else begins again, and it blossoms in the summer,
filling the afternoons and evenings, and then as soon
as the chill rains come, it stops and leaves you to face
the fall alone.
—A. BARTLETT GIAMATTI

✦✦

➤ Quick guys get tired; big guys don't shrink.
—MARV HARSHMAN

✦✦✦

Holiday

Christmas is the Disneyfication of Christianity.
—DON CUPITT

++

Christmas is a race to see which gives out first—your
money or your feet.
—ANONYMOUS

+++

A Christmas shopper's complaint is one of long-
standing.
—JAY LENO

++

For those of you out there who are thinking about
the Hanukkah-versus-Christmas thing, let me tell
you this: Quite honestly—and this comes from
an experiment with a two-and-a-half-year-old—
Christmas *blows the doors* off of Hanukkah.
—JON STEWART

+++

Hanukkah Books You'll Never See

> **The Schmuck Who Stole Hanukkah:** The story of a moron that tries to enter the village of Schvantzville to steal all the toys but can't seem to pick the "big" night.

> **Good Night, Moon-orah:** A very *short* book, it follows a child on each night as she says good night to her presents. Chapter 1: "Good Night, Dreidel." End of chapter. Chapter 2: "Good Night, Chocolate Gelt in a Mesh Bag." End of chapter. And so on.

> **The Runaway Dreidel:** A dreidel wants to run away because everyone thinks he's just a cheap little top with writing on it.

> **The Giving Tree (But Just a Little):** A children's book that is instructional for parents, it tells the story of a little Jewish boy who befriends a tree and is institutionalized for it.

> **The Big Book of Mackabee Pop-ups:** Oy, too many swords. You'll put your eye out.

Really Bad Holiday Ideas

1. Christmas ads with smoking Santas

2. Xmas cards with naked pics of you and family

3. Gifting a mausoleum for Christmas (just $10,000!)

4. Musical holly/wreaths/poinsettias

5. Mistletoe belt

The three wise men sound very generous, but what you've got to remember is that those gifts were joint Christmas and birthday presents.
—JIMMY CARR
♦♦

Christmas: A day set apart and consecrated to gluttony, drunkenness, maudlin sentiment, gift-taking, public dullness, and domestic behavior.
—AMBROSE BIERCE
♦♦♦

12 Days of Gifts

1. Islamic Poker[70]

2. Fairly Serious Putty

3. The Lil' Electrical Outlet Licker

4. 5200 Card Pickup: a card game that keeps the kids busy all day

5. Ginsu Boomerang

6. The Pee-wee Herman Pull Toy

7. Nintendo 63 (This one was pretty easy to come by this holiday, for some reason.)

8. Hasbro's Lil' Barber

9. Tickle Me Carrot Top

10. Angry Birds-Baked-in-a-Pie

11. Doggie Dentist kit

12. The screenplay to the last *Star Trek* movie—"Live Long Then Expire"

---

[70] Lose a hand? Lose a hand!

Christmas Facts

➢ A Christmas club, a savings account in which a person deposits a fixed amount of money regularly to be used at Christmas for shopping, came about around 1905. It is now a source of much amusement for bank employees when you get your passbook and realize you could have made more interest with a lemonade stand.

➢ According to a 1995 survey, 7 out of 10 British dogs get Christmas gifts from their doting owners. That same survey revealed that only 5 of those 10 dogs actually return those gifts for something else.

➢ Although many believe the Friday after Thanksgiving is the busiest shopping day of the year, it is not. It is the fifth to tenth busiest day. It is, however, the day when the murder rate goes up significantly in almost forty states.

It's That Time of Year Again

- ↔ "Merry Christmas"—not "Happy holidays" or "Season's Greetings"—is once again okay to use.

- ↔ "Family trees"? Or worse, "holiday trees"? Not on my watch.

- ↔ What about Christmas songs? "Have Yourself a Merry Little Day of Winter"? "Frosty the Snowperson"? Or "Deck the Halls with Boughs of Unendangered Foliage"?

- ↔ You couldn't give a "bum" a handout for "the holidays" anymore . . . no, no, he's a *displaced person.*

- ↔ "Gee, Daddy, Santa Claus is really fat!" . . . "No, sweetie, he's got an *enlarged physical condition caused by a completely natural genetically induced hormonal imbalance.*"

- ↔ "Look, Mom, an elf!" . . . "Now, now, that man is just *vertically challenged.*"

↪ Tip the janitor? No, no, no . . . he's a *custodial artist*. Double whatever you were gonna give him.

↪ Go ahead, say what you want, because it's beginning to feel a lot like that short period of time in December.

I have long thought it a pity that Scrooge, like so many people in Dickens, spoilt his case by overstatement. To dismiss the Christmas spirit as humbug will not quite do as it stands, but it gets close.
—KINGSLEY AMIS

✦✦✦

Oh, joy . . . Christmas Eve. By this time tomorrow, millions of people, knee-deep in tinsel and wrapping paper, will utter those heartfelt words, "Is this all I got?"
—FRASIER

✦✦

In the immortal words of Tiny Tim, "God help us everyone!"
—GROUCHO MARX

++

Most Texans think Hanukkah is some sort of duck call.
—RICHARD LEWIS

+++

Brain Scan: Inside the Head of a Snowman

> ➤ I'm dreaming of a white Christmas . . .
> I'm dreaming of a white Christmas . . .
> I'm dreaming of a white Christmas . . .
>
> ➤ I'm dreaming of a white Christmas . . .
> I'm dreaming of a white Christmas . . .
> I'm dreaming of a white Christmas . . .
>
> ➤ I'm dreaming of a white Christmas . . .
> I'm dreaming of a white Christmas . . .
> I'm dreaming of a white Christmas . . .

Jeez, why are we talking about God and religion? It's
Christmas!
—*ROSEANNE*

✦✦✦

Roses are reddish / Violets are bluish / If it weren't for
Christmas / We'd all be Jewish.
—BENNY HILL

✦✦

Christmas Facts

➤ "Hot cockles" was a popular game at Christmas in medieval times. It was a game in which the other players took turns striking the blindfolded player, who had to guess the name of the person delivering each blow. Hot cockles was still a Christmas pastime until the Victorian era and has only recently been reintroduced as a method of preparation for holiday shopping.

➤ According to the National Christmas Tree Association, Americans buy 37.1 million real Christmas trees each year. On January 2, the National Waste Management Association claims it picks up almost 36.9 million of said trees.

➤ After *A Christmas Carol*, Charles Dickens wrote several other Christmas stories, one each year, but none were as successful as the original. Among the least successful were *A Christmas Mildred*, *A Christmas Agnes*, and *A*

Christmas Bob. Additionally, before settling on the name Tiny Tim, Dickens considered three other alliterative names: Little Larry, Puny Pete, Small Sam, Miniscule Marty, Wee Willie, and Malnourished Mark. Never had a chance.

➤ An average household in America will mail out 28 Christmas cards each year and see 28 cards return in their place. Because if you get 27 back this year, you're mailing out 27 cards next year.

When you compare Christmas to Hanukkah, Christmas is great. Hanukkah sucks! First night you get socks. Second night, an eraser, a notebook. It's a Back-to-School holiday!
—LEWIS BLACK

✦✦✦

December 25 is National Jews Go to the Movies Day.
—JON STEWART

++

On the first night of Hanukkah, Jewish parents do
something that can only be described as sadistic
when they hand their child a top. A top. To play
with. They call this top a dreidel. I know a fuckin' top
when I see one. You can call it the king's nuts, I don't
give a shit. Call it whatever you like, it's a top. A top
is not something you play with. A top is not a toy. A
toy is something you participate with. It'd be like the
equivalent of if you had a young girl and she wanted a
Barbie and you handed her a stick and said
give it a name.
—LEWIS BLACK

+++

Christmas: Holiday in which the past or the future
are not of as much interest as the present.

++

Christmas is a holiday that persecutes the lonely, the
frayed, and the rejected.
—JIMMY CANNON

+++

If you want to restore your faith in humanity,
think about Christmas. If you want to destroy it
again, think about Christmas shopping. But the
gifts aren't the important thing about the holidays.
The important thing is having your family around
resenting you.
—RENO GOODALE

++

Four Reasons Hanukkah Sucks

1. **No good cards**: Rows and rows of Christmas cards and only one row of Hanukkah cards. Yeah, like you've got a hundred different people you want to send Hanukkah cards to . . . well, you'd better get them out in time because, after all, there are only EIGHT DAYS ON WHICH THEY CAN BE DELIVERED. The best Hanukkah card ever? "It's not your fault that Hanukkah sucks." End of story.

2. **The name**: Too many ways to spell and pronounce the name of the holiday. Yeah, I know. It's hard to say. Sounds funny, too. Like you've got something stuck in your throat. And oy, boychick, is it hard to spell. Gee, is it *Hanukah* or *Chanuka* or *Chanukah* or *Chanukkah* or *Channukah* or *Hanukah* or *Hannukah* or *Hanukkah* or *Hanuka* or *Hanukka* or *Hanaka* or *Haneka* or *Hanika* or *Khanukkah* . . . Please kill me now?

3. **Bad gifts**: Small. Large. Two medium. Small again. Large. Nothing. Small. Large(ish). Let's face it, Jewish parents don't really have much imagination.

Not their fault. They've been struggling forever in the shadow of the Big One. For years. Their parents had the same problem. It's up to you to stop the madness.

4. **The music**: I once heard a story that Irving Berlin hated "White Christmas." Whattya wanna bet that rumor got started by somebody who was pissed off that the only music associated with this holiday are a lame Adam Sandler ditty that's just dumb . . . and the dreidel song.

A holiday is when you celebrate something that's all finished up, that happened a long time ago and now there's nothing left to celebrate but the dead.
—ABRAHAM POLONSKY

♦♦

The only way to spend New Year's Eve is either quietly with friends or in a brothel. Otherwise, when the evening ends and people pair off, someone is bound to be left in tears.
—W. H. AUDEN

♦♦♦

~✦~

A Bubbie was giving directions to her grown grandson, who was coming to visit for Chanukah with his wife.

"You come to the front door of the apartment complex. You'll see a big panel at the door. With your elbow push button 14T. I will buzz you in."

"Okay, got it."

"No, there's more. When you come inside, the elevator is on the right. Get in and with your elbow hit 14. When you get out, I am on the left. With your elbow, hit my doorbell."

"Grandma, that sounds easy," replied the grandson, "but why am I hitting all these buttons with my elbow?"

To which she answered, "What, you're coming empty-handed?"

~✦~

6 Festive Ways to Drive Your Family Crazy

> Go to the mall with your mom and sit on Santa's lap. Refuse to get off.

> Claim you were a Christmas tree in your former life. When your dad tries to bring one into the room, scream bloody murder and thrash on the floor.

> Hang a stocking with your sister's name on it and fill it with coal. When she asks, say, "You've been very naughty this year."

> Build a snowman with your brother and place a hat on its head. If it doesn't come to life, start crying, "It didn't work!"

> Stand in front of the mirror reciting "How the Grinch Stole Christmas" over and over in your underwear.

> Wake up the house every morning by singing, "He sees you when you're sleeping . . ."

My parents, my whole life, combined my birthday with Christmas, and you know how frustrating that is for a child—especially as I was born in July.
—RITA RUDNER

✦✦✦

Last Christmas, I gave my kid a BB gun. He gave me a sweatshirt with a bull's-eye on the back.
—RODNEY DANGERFIELD

✦✦

Thanksgiving. It's like we didn't even try to come up with a tradition. The tradition is, we overeat. "Hey, how about at Thanksgiving we just eat a lot?" "But we do that every day!" "Oh. What if we eat a lot with people that annoy the hell out of us?"
—JIM GAFFIGAN

✦✦✦

It is customarily said that Christmas is done "for the kids." Considering how awful Christmas is and how little our society likes children, this must be true.
—P. J. O'ROURKE

✦✦

Santa Claus has the right idea. Visit people once a year.
—VICTOR BORGE

✦✦✦

Thanksgiving is an emotional time. People travel thousands of miles to be with the people they see only once a year. And then discover that once a year is way too often.
—JOHNNY CARSON

✦✦

~✦~

Kevin: I got myself for Secret Santa. I was supposed to tell somebody, but I didn't.

Michael: Presents are the best way to show someone how much you care. It's like this tangible thing that you can point to and say, "Hey man, I love you this many dollars" worth.

So Phyllis is basically saying, "Hey, Michael, I know you did a lot to help the office this year, but I only care about you a homemade oven mitt's worth." I gave Ryan an iPod.

Everyone wants the iPod. It's a huge hit. It is almost a Christmas miracle.

Dwight: Michael keeps bragging about his iPod. But you know what? Two paintball lessons with someone as experienced as I am is worth easily, like, two grand.

Michael: Unbelievable. I do the nicest thing that anyone has ever done for these people, and they freak out. Well, happy birthday, Jesus. Sorry your party's so lame.

—THE OFFICE

~✦~

"You mean you're going to send the same form letter to the Great Pumpkin, Santa Claus, and the Easter Bunny?" "Why not? These guys get so much mail they can't possibly tell the difference . . . I bet they don't even read the letters themselves! How could they? The trouble with you, Charlie Brown, is you don't understand how these big organizations work!"
—LUCY, *CHARLIE BROWN*

♦♦♦

Santa and his reindeer land on top of an outhouse. Santa looks around for a moment, and then yells "No, Rudolph! I said the SCHMIDT house!"
—ANONYMOUS

~♦~

Q: How do elves greet each other?
A: Small world, isn't it?

~♦~

Santa Claus? You have to look very carefully at a man like this. He comes but once a year? Down the chimney? And in my sock?
—IRWIN COREY

♦♦♦

Top 10 Responses to the Gift of a Holiday Sweater

10. Hey! Now there's a gift!

9. Well, well, well . . .

8. Boy, if I had not recently shot up four sizes, that would've fit.

7. This is perfect for wearing around the basement.

6. I hope this never catches fire! It is fire season, though. There are lots of unexplained fires.

5. If the dog buries it, I'll be furious!

4. I love it—but I fear the jealousy it will inspire.

3. Sadly, tomorrow I enter the Federal Witness Protection Program.

2. Damn . . . I got this the year I vowed to give all my gifts to charity.

1. I really don't deserve this.

Santa Pickup Lines

> ➤ Wanna see my twelve-inch elf?

> ➤ I've got something special in the sack for you!

> ➤ Ever make it with a fat guy with a whip?

> ➤ I know when you've been bad or good, so let's skip the small talk.

> ➤ Some of my best toys run on batteries . . .

> ➤ Interested in seeing the "North Pole"? (Well, that's what the Mrs. calls it.)

> ➤ I see you when you're sleeping . . . and you don't wear any underwear, do you?

> ➤ Screw the "nice" list—I've got you on my "naughty" list!

> ➤ Wanna join the "Mile High" Club?

> ➤ That's not a candy cane in my pocket, honey. I'm just glad to see you . . .

WAYS TO CONFUSE SANTA

➢ Instead of milk and cookies, leave him a salad and a note explaining that you think he could stand to lose a few pounds.

➢ While he's in the house, go find his sleigh and write him a speeding ticket.

➢ Leave him a note explaining that you've gone away for the holidays. Ask if he would mind watering your plants.

➢ While he's in the house, replace all his reindeer with exact replicas. Then wait and see what happens when he tries to get them to fly.

➢ Keep an angry bull in your living room. If you think a bull goes crazy when he sees a little red cape, wait until he sees that big red Santa suit!

➢ Build an army of mean-looking snowmen on the roof, holding signs that say "We hate Christmas" and "Go away Santa."

➢ Leave a note by the telephone telling Santa that Mrs. Claus called and wanted to remind him to pick up some milk and a loaf of bread on his way home.

➢ Throw a surprise party for Santa when he comes down the chimney. Refuse to let him leave until the strippers arrive.

➢ While he's in the house, find the sleigh and sit in it. As soon as he comes back and sees you, tell him that he shouldn't have missed that last payment, and take off.

➢ Leave a plate filled with cookies and a glass of milk out, with a note that says, "For The Tooth Fairy. :)" Leave another plate out with half a stale cookie and a few drops of skim milk in a dirty glass with a note that says, "For Santa. :("

➢ Take everything out of your house as if it's just been robbed. When Santa arrives, show up dressed like a policeman and say, "Well, well. They always return to the scene of the crime."

➢ Leave out a copy of your Christmas list with last-minute changes and corrections.

➢ While he's in the house, cover the top of the chimney with barbed wire.

➢ Leave lots of hunting trophies and guns out where Santa's sure to see them. Go outside, yell, "Ooh!

Look! A deer! And he's got a red nose!" and fire a gun.

➤ Leave Santa a note explaining that you've moved. Include a map with unclear and hard-to-read directions to your new house.

➤ Set a bear trap at the bottom of the chimney. Wait for Santa to get caught in it, and then explain that you're sorry, but that from a distance he looked like a bear.

➤ Leave out a Santa suit with a dry-cleaning bill.

➤ Paint "hoof-prints" all over your face and clothes. While he's in the house, go out on the roof. When he comes back up, act like you've been "trampled." Threaten to sue.

➤ Instead of ornaments, decorate your tree with Easter eggs.

Department Store Santa's Pet Peeves

➢ Kids who refuse to believe that it's fruitcake on your breath and not gin

➢ When the last guy to use the beard leaves bits of his lunch in it

➢ Even with the costume, people keep recognizing you from Crime Watch

➢ Parents who get all uptight when you offer their kids a swig from your hip flask

➢ Enduring the taunts of your old buddies from drama school

➢ Those dorks in the Power Rangers costumes get all the babes

➢ Kids who don't understand that Santa's been a little jittery since he got back from 'Nam

➢ Two words: lap rash

Top Reindeer Games

- Strip poker with Mrs. Claus
- Attach the Mistletoe to Santa's Ass
- Spin the Salt Lick
- Crapping down the chimneys of nonbelievers
- Moose or Dare
- Bait-and-Shoot Elmo
- Turn-Frosty-Yellow-from-50-Paces
- Scare the Holy Crap Out of the Airline Pilot
- Convince the Elves to Eat Raisinets
- Pin the Tail on Santa's Big Fat Animal-Abusing Ass
- Hide the Venison Sausage with Vixen
- Elf Tossing
- Sniff the Tail on the Donkey
- The "Rudolph the Shitfaced Reindeer" Drinking Game

Top 10 Reasons to Like Hanukkah

1. No roof damage from Santa and his reindeer.

2. Never a silent night when you're among your Jewish loved ones.

3. If someone screws up on their gift, there are seven more days to correct it.

4. You can use your fireplace.

5. Naked Spin-the-Dreidel.

6. Fun waxy buildup on the menorah.

7. No awkward explanations of virgin birth.

8. Cheer? Optional.

9. No Irving Berlin songs.

10. Betting Hanukkah gelt on candle races.

Santa is a genuinely sinister figure. Think about it: a single, old man watches everything little children do, because he wants to know which are the naughty ones? People have been hounded out of town by mobs for far less.
—JULIAN BAGGINI

✦✦✦

In the old days, it was not called the Holiday Season; the Christians called it "Christmas" and went to church; the Jews called it "Hanukkah" and went to synagogue; the atheists went to parties and drank. People passing each other on the street would say "Merry Christmas!" or "Happy Hanukkah!" or (to the atheists) "Look out for the wall!"
—DAVE BARRY

✦✦

Christmas is a time for remembering. So that's me, f**ked.
—OZZY OSBOURNE

✦✦✦

Thanksgiving is a magical time of year when families across the country join together to raise America's obesity statistics. Personally, I love Thanksgiving traditions: watching football, making pumpkin pie, and saying the magic phrase that sends your aunt storming out of the dining room to sit in her car.
—STEPHEN COLBERT

++

Thanksgiving, man . . . Not a good day to be my pants.
—KEVIN JAMES

+++

If you're at a Thanksgiving dinner, but you don't like the stuffing or the cranberry sauce or anything else, just pretend like you're eating it, but instead, put it all in your lap and form it into a big mushy ball. Then, later, when you're out back having cigars with the boys, let out a big fake cough and throw the ball to the ground. Then say, "Boy, these are good cigars!"
—JACK HANDEY

++

Christmas is a major holiday. Chanukah is a minor holiday with the same theme as most Jewish holidays. They tried to kill us, we survived, let's eat.
—ANONYMOUS

+++

Next to the presidency, detrimming a tree has to be the loneliest job in the world. It has fallen to women for centuries and is considered a skill only they can do, like replacing the roll on the toilet tissue spindle, painting baseboards, holding a wet washcloth for a child who is throwing up, or taking out a splinter with a needle.
—ERMA BOMBECK

++

The day after Christmas: when we all have two more ugly sweaters.
—CRAIG KILBORN

+++

Conclusion

"And in the end, the snark you take is equal to the snark you make."

Those are the words I ended my first book (*The Snark Handbook: A Reference Guide to Verbal Sparring*) with, taking Paul McCartney's existentialist poetry and pompously changing the words . . . and haven't heard a word from the remaining fabs yet. Why haven't I? Fear of snark.

Snark is a tool. Yes, the ability to snark can change your life. (Not really, but it looks good as I type it out on the computer.) It can diffuse a tense situation or it can "fuse" one.

Your choice.

All you need to do is follow a few simple rules:

1. Snark fast. When the opportunity presents itself, jump in.
2. Snark hard. Pull no punches.
3. Snark last. The final word is the best word.

And when these few rules fail, follow the advice of Teddy Roosevelt . . . carry a really big stick.

Stay snarky.

LD